Classroom Cinema

Richard A. Maynard

Teachers College, Columbia University
New York and London

This book is dedicated to my family—Lorrie, Jeffrey, and Kevin Maynard and Sue and Gene Maynard.

Copyright © 1977 by Richard A. Maynard. All rights reserved. Published by Teachers College Press, 1234 Amsterdam Avenue, New York, NY 10027

COVER AND DESIGN BY FRANK MEDINA

Library of Congress Cataloging in Publication Data

Maynard, Richard A
  Classroom cinema.

  Filmography: p.
  Bibliography: p.
  Includes index.
  1. Moving-pictures in education. 2. Moving-pictures — Catalogs. I. Title.
LB1044.M363   371.33'523   77-21653
ISBN 0-8077-2540-4

MANUFACTURED IN THE U.S.A.

Contents

Acknowledgments

A book of this kind is not possible without the assistance and encouragement of a great many people. I would like to personally thank the following friends and colleagues: film industry "lions" Doug Lemza of Films Inc., Adam Reilly of Time-Life Films, Leo Dratfield of Phoenix Films and later Films Inc., Walter Dauler of Macmillan Audio Brandon Films, Len Fazzio of Universal 16, Donald Krim of United Artists 16, Alan Twyman of Twyman Films, and Elaine Mason of Learning Corporation of America; professional screen educators David Mallery, John Culkin, David Sohn, John Geogeghan, Frank McLaughlin, Kit Laybourne, and Ron Sutton; editorial colleagues Loretta Marion, Lois Markham and Pat Fingeroth of *Scholastic Teacher* (I forgive you all for cutting my masterful prose), Mary Allison, former editor of Citation Press, Bill Cook and Bob Boynton of Hayden Book Co., and Dick Robinson, president and publisher of Scholastic, Inc., who kept the faith.

Richard A. Maynard

The Genesis of a
Movie Teacher:
An Introduction

In the summer of 1967 I became a teacher. I had functioned under the label "teacher" for two previous years, performing such expected and acceptable tasks as lecturing, conducting (and generally monopolizing) class discussions, applying audio-visual aids (filmstrips, transparencies, slides—all of maps and charts, of course), giving tests, grading papers, and handing out countless platitudes of adult advice to the "culturally deprived" adolescents in my charge. As I look back on myself in the classroom from 1965 to 1967, I realize I would have qualified for a villain's role in Frederick Wiseman's scathing documentary film *High School.*

But by the spring of '67 I had become rudely sensitized to my own pedagogical shortcomings. The rebellious sixties were in full swing, particularly in the black ghetto of North Philadelphia where I worked. Student sit-ins, boycotts, protests, and cries for "meaningful" education permeated the walls of the old prison where I was assigned to work. Simon Gratz High School had become a cauldron of black student protest. "Relevance" (or "revelance" as many students defiantly mispronounced it) became a fourth R in urban education. And I, as a militant group of my students accused me, was "irrevelant" (sic).

This was a bitter pill to swallow, but it was true. In the mid-sixties, the teaching profession suddenly found itself full of new blood—young, well-educated, often disillusioned academics who "dropped in" to teaching on the way to discovering themselves. Their motives may have been material—a paying job while finishing graduate studies or supporting a husband or wife who was in professional school—or pragmatic (idealistic), since urban ghetto teaching generally qualified young males for a 2A draft deferment and an alternative to Canadian citizenship. (My motives were a combination of all of these.) The exposure of these white, middle-class disillusioned souls to black America was to have a radicalizing effect.

Those of us who stayed for the confrontation came to realize that the accusations leveled against us were a challenge, a personal dare to see if we really could apply all the benefits of our education to a community that had been severely shortchanged by the Great Society.

Sweet Inspiration

This brings me back to where I started in my first sentence—the summer of 1967. During my second year in the classroom I came into contact with a great man, as did just about everyone involved in the Philadelphia school system. Marcus Foster had been a product of that system. This husky, affable, absolutely charming man had a knack for eloquence and inspirational leadership that put him in a league with Martin Luther King, and made him the Sidney Poitier of urban education. Yet, he had grown up a South Philly street kid, and this gave him the sense of hard pragmatism that made him so effective in dealing with kids and teachers. To the students he was one of them who'd made good, but who never gave them the black bourgeois "up from slavery" bit. He knew their jargon, understood their values and, most of all, believed in them as human beings.

To teachers (many of whom were initially skeptical of his identification with the kids), he offered the fullest opportunities to develop our potential. He encouraged us to develop courses and materials that went beyond the limitations of the assigned curriculum. If any of us knew anything about black American history, African geography, or other subjects with high student interest appeal, we were encouraged to teach them. Since I had some background in these areas (a few college courses), he had me develop an elective in black history—the first ever offered in the Philadelphia school system.

But Marcus wasn't just interested in some limited black parochial education. He believed—as I now believe—that an education is an all-encompassing cultural experience. Our goals were not just to teach a lot of hip, entertaining courses in the name of relevance (which too often became the case in the 60s). Reading, writing, correct public speaking, political savvy, personal economics, and art, music, and literary appreciation (from Hughes and Ellington to Shakespeare and Stravinsky) were our real academic goals. To Marcus Foster it was all a matter of providing exciting vehicles toward these ends. "We are in the business of education," he used to say in one of his standard inspirational speeches, "and in business you have to compete to win over your customers."

I didn't quite realize then that the "customers" he spoke of winning over included teachers as well as students.

A Medium and a Method
In June 1967 I had reached a personal crossroads in my own teaching career. I'd been preparing to quit and finish the

remaining credits toward my Ph.D., though the past few months had been among the most exciting of my life. Then Marcus offered me and fourteen other faculty members an interesting form of summer employment. Fifteen NDEA fellowships were being given to our faculty to enable them to spend the summer at Princeton University developing innovative curriculum. The fellowship included six graduate credits and a healthy stipend. Considering the kinds of summer jobs available for young teachers in those days, I jumped at the chance, though I was still not totally sure about my future in public education. A summer at Princeton seemed infinitely preferable to chauffeuring eight-year-olds to day camp or selling magazine subscriptions.

The Princeton experience actually did change my life. Marcus had primed me for it and made me aware of my potential as a teacher, but that summer I came to believe that I was one.

The Trenton-Princeton Institute, as the experience was officially called, was a two-phased program for teachers. Each morning we were assigned to team teaching situations at Trenton (New Jersey) High School. There were three of us to a team, under the leadership of a master teacher, who, we were told, was an expert in his or her field. (Actually, the expertise of these masters varied tremendously, though the fellow I worked under, Tom Koberna from Cleveland, was an incredibly gifted teacher.) Our students consisted of groups of recently returned dropouts, many of whom had serious emotional as well as academic problems. Quite a few were in this program as part of their legal probation.

Our afternoons, and some evenings, were spent in the academic cloisters on the Princeton campus where we had seminars with our master teachers and a wide variety of learning experts. In the initial days of the program, we were encouraged to suggest any method or approach we would like to try, regardless of the budgetary or administrative prohibitions against them in our regular classrooms. The federal government, which sponsored the program, had allocated enough money for any of us to experiment with a dream curriculum for the next six weeks. It was beyond belief. The previous year I had to buy blank ditto masters with my own money, and suddenly was told I had an unlimited budget. Shock set in. Neither I nor my colleagues could come up with the slightest idea of what we wanted to do, so for the first week or so, our master teachers did most of the expensive experimenting.

The master teacher in charge of my group declared he was going to rent a film to kick off a series of lessons on law and authority. Up to that point my whole association with films in the classroom was a negative one. As a student I had been subjected to countless "educational" films, including such standards as *The Honey Bee's Domain, The Great American Eagle,* and *How to Catch a Cold,* a film Walt Disney made for the U.S. Board of Health right after World War II. I remember being herded into cavernous auditoriums and told to sit in silence while I watched a postage stamp image on a screen and listened to a sour, tinny sound track. At least the experience offered a good opportunity for daydreaming.

As a teacher during the previous two years, I had deliberately stayed away from films. My less energetic colleagues would show 16mm films—usually old TV documentaries—anytime they were available from the Board of Education's audio-visual department. Usually it didn't even matter what the film was. The attitude traditionally among teachers up to that time was (and maybe still is), "If it's in the building, show it." I even allowed a colleague of mine to lure my classes into his room to see a film about the Federal Reserve System, which I had taught about recently. My students' reactions confirmed my suspicions about such visual aids. They slept.

So, when I found out that an initial sum from our limitless budget was being spent for a film, I became a little skeptical. Then I found out that the class was going to see *On the Waterfront*.

The class screened the film during the first two-thirds of the morning session. (A benefit of the self-contained morning period was that we could keep the kids in the same room long enough to view a feature film. I'll have more to say about alternatives to this later in the book.) For the remainder of the session we formed a large rap group to discuss the ethical problems confronting Marlon Brando in the film. Should he have testified against his former buddies, including his own brother?

As I've said, the kids in this class weren't exactly serious students. All of them had police records, and they'd lived through all kinds of personal hell—jail, drugs, gang fights. It was hard to believe that the oldest of them wasn't yet seventeen. But at this moment, in this group, they were taking school very seriously. Their comments were thoughtful and personal. Everyone had an opinion and expressed it. The four teachers barely said a word. That night we asked the students to put their thoughts on paper, . . . to just continue the rap in a kind of story form. Don't worry about spelling, punctuation, for now anyway. Just express yourselves on paper.

The next day we saw the results. The papers weren't grammatically pretty, and the spelling was atrocious, but they were full of words; it was the first written work many had produced in years.

It began to dawn on me that films like *On the Waterfront*—good, entertaining commercial movies—presented a fantastic opportunity to open new lines of communication between kids and teachers. The movie could be—and in this case was—the catalyst, the vehicle Marcus Foster was talking about. We used *On the Waterfront* as part of a unit on law and authority. It stood up well as a source to build discussion

On The Waterfront

around and as a stimulus to some creative writing. It also led to some outside reading.

The movie buff in me emerged, and I began to think of other films I liked that could be used in similar situations. During the rest of the summer my colleagues and I used such movies as *A Raisin in the Sun, The Loneliness of the Long-Distance Runner, Night and Fog,* and *The Ox-Bow Incident* to teach social studies and English units on family life, personal values, and the judicial system. At the same time the films were encouraging reading, writing, and speaking among some very reluctant learners. The films weren't visual aids any more—they were primary classroom sources.

Putting It in Writing

When I returned to my school in the fall, I planned an entire year's humanities program for English and social studies around a series of themes such as those we used during the summer. *All* I needed was the money for film rentals and paperback books. "No way," I thought, as I devised my dream curriculum. The federal boondoggle was over. But Marcus Foster appreciated the fact that I thought I had learned something, and he helped me to secure a special innovative teaching grant from the Philadelphia Board of Education (which later became a city-wide policy, incidentally) to fund my program. He then gave me another bit of advice about how to keep my program going if it was successful. "Publicize it. Document every success. Save student papers, tape discussions, invite colleagues, administrators, politicians into the classes. Write about it!"*

The rest is history. I wrote several articles on my experiences over the next few years in *The Social Studies, Media and Methods* and *Scholastic Teacher.* These in turn led to a book, *The Celluloid Curriculum* (Hayden Book Company, 1970), and a follow-up series of student books, *Film: Attitudes and Issues* (1972–74). In 1970 I began writing a monthly column on film teaching in *Scholastic Teacher,* based mostly on my previous month's classroom experiences. In that column I tried to communicate about the use of commercial film as a valuable classroom tool. I have never stressed, in all these years, the concept of film study for its own sake. Certainly there are great artistic aspects to filmmaking that need to be recognized by students, and there are a few superb film artists whose individual contributions to the medium must be pointed out (see the chapter on John Ford). But, with a few

---

*I must note here that taking his own advice the career of this great individual blossomed during the next few years. He became Associate Superintendent of Schools in Philadelphia in 1969. In 1971 he was named Superintendent of Schools for Oakland, California, where he was known for his innovative approaches and humanistic leadership. It is one of the great tragedies of our time that in November 1974 Marcus Foster was murdered by a group of self-styled radical headline grabbers called The Symbionese Liberation Army (SLA). For me, this has always been American education's cruelest loss.

exceptions, I have always devoted my teaching and writing to the application of film toward other ends—the teaching of history, literature, writing, or mass communication. In addition, I have consistently tried to emphasize the impact of the film medium on the lives of my students. The ability to read moving images is almost a survival tool in today's society. A wide critical exposure to the mass media, particularly film, in the classroom helps provide that survival tool.

This book is a collection of classroom experiences and reminiscences of my film teaching career since that critical summer of 1967. Several of the chapters originally appeared in a more abbreviated form as columns in *Scholastic Teacher*. The book is part memoir and part guide. My film selections are, for the most part, commercial movies, many the products of Hollywood. The contexts I have chosen for these films, as I've already explained, are not based on the advancement of cinematic art. Because of this, my film selections throughout the book are highly subjective, representing my own feelings about what will "work" in a classroom of teen-agers and what will not.

It is my hope that the suggestions the book provides will help to foster a whole new generation of movie teachers. Although I'm no longer a full-time high school teacher, I am heavily involved in teacher training in the graduate courses I teach at The Center for Understanding Media in New York. I realize that the economic problems of the seventies and their effects on schools mean that efforts toward any kind of more innovative education will be difficult. In addition, cries of "Back to basics" and well-meaning (if misguided) community pressures on teachers may make some wince at suggestions in this book. But for me, the medium has always been the *method,* not necessarily the *message;* film is as valuable a tool in teaching the "basics" as I have ever found. If this book, and indeed my entire teaching career, has a goal, it is that screen education should be an inseparable part of acceptable classroom practice.

In his definitive study of American education in the 60s, *Crisis in the Classroom,* Charles Silberman put this very well when he concluded:

There is enormous grumbling, to be sure, about the corrupting effects of television, advertising, and the mass media in general, but painfully little thought about how these media affect youngsters, let alone how the schools might take account of them. This failure is bound up with teachers' and administrators' inability or reluctance to recognize that we are no longer living in a purely literary culture, that the current generation will get a large proportion of its information and values from films, television and radio, and that they therefore need to be taught to deal critically with nonliterary as well as literary forms.*

Crisis in the Classroom (New York: Random House, 1970), p. 186.

1

Getting into Film— A Basic Guide for Classroom Teachers

1

Overcoming the Headaches: Funding and Scheduling an Effective Film Program

The more I talk to fellow social studies and English teachers, the more convinced I become of their tremendous interest in movie-oriented curriculum. I have rarely seen teachers more enthusiastic about classroom method.

"You mean *Dr. Strangelove* is available in 16mm? Fantastic! What distributor has it? How long is the rental waiting list? Oh, I can't wait to use it in my unit on social satire. . . ."

This is typical of the initial reaction of many interested teachers. And then reality sets in.

"Oh, by the way, how much does it cost to rent? And, how can I show a 95-minute film in my class when it only lasts 45 minutes? Maybe they'll show it on television soon."

Without a doubt, one of the biggest drawbacks for teachers who want to use films in their classrooms is lack of funds available for film rentals. This is a problem I struggled with for all seven of my years teaching high school, and one

I'm still struggling with in my college course in screen education. I have no panaceas to offer for this difficulty. As long as administrators and curriculum specialists refuse to give motion pictures the academic legitimacy they deserve, money for this area will continue to be tight. However, those who genuinely want to get into film teaching needn't totally despair. There are some ways of easing the money problems. Having resorted to all of them at one time or another, let me offer some suggestions.

Sources of Funds and Alternatives

School or Department Audio-Visual Budgets

Every school, even the most destitute (like the Philadelphia one I taught in) sets aside some annual amount of money for the purchase or rental of A-V materials. Each teacher is usually entitled to a slice of this budget (no matter how small), and it would be appropriate to request that one's share be allocated to rent a feature film. If the funds are skimpy, or if you want a film with a high rental rate, two or three interested teachers could pool their allotments and combine classes to show the film.

Many schools already have some special budgets for film rentals. This is particularly true of English departments with extensive elective programs. Most of the time this money is spent on some "supplementary" movie shown during an extended assembly program and having little relationship to actual curriculum. My suggestion is to divert the film budget away from such mass screenings, which generally have little transfer value for the classroom (we all know how seriously kids take assemblies), into the hands of a few enterprising teachers who have planned for a program of movies directly tied in with their classroom activities. Such a procedure is actually more economical, since most 16mm distributors charge considerably lower rental rates for films viewed by audiences of under 100 students. For example, a major distributor might rent a popular film at a base rate of $50 for a group of less than 100 students. The same film costs $100 for an assembly showing to 251 to 500 students. Wouldn't one or two classes specifically studying the subject matter of the film benefit far more from seeing it in the intimacy of a classroom, than half the student body herded into a large auditorium? And, with the money saved a few teachers can rent additional films suitable for their curricula.

The point is that most schools have some flexibility in how they spend their A-V funds. Enterprising teachers should try to persuade their administrations to divert some money for classroom film study.

The Book Fund

All schools allocate budgets for replenishing book supplies each semester. I am not suggesting that teachers steal funds from the literary "nuts and bolts" of their schools to rent movies, nor am I implying that any administration should substitute film rentals for book purchases. I do think, though, that teachers can spend a part of their share of this source of funds on films. Today many high schools are using more and more paperback sets of books. In a unit on propaganda, a class may use 30 paperback copies of Vance Packard's *The Hidden Persuaders* and 30 copies of George Orwell's *1984* (both sets costing about $60). If there is money in the budget for a third source, a class could really comprehend the nature of propaganda by seeing Leni Riefensthal's diabolically brilliant film *Triumph of the Will,* which the Nazi's used in 1933 to sell themselves to the German people. This costs about $50 for a basic rental, and although it can only be shown once, most sets of paperback books don't usually last beyond one class reading either. It seems reasonable that a part of the book fund (however small) can be allocated for relevant films.

Outside Grants

My first source of funds for a year of teaching with films came from a useful incentive program of the Philadelphia Board of Education. The Board made available a small number of special teacher grants for innovative programs for classroom experimentation. I proposed a course using films as literary sources and requested $600 to fund it. I was awarded a grant of $350, which is just about what I needed for the course. (Please note: *Always request more.* Think big.)

Several school systems still maintain grant programs, though there are always more applicants than recipients. Check to see if yours has one. If your school system has no such policy, suggest one. You have nothing to lose.

In my travels around the country as Scholastic's editorial director for language arts, I have met several English teachers who are running innovative elective courses in film and mass media communications, as well as in thematic and generic areas, with funds for films provided by their state councils on the arts. Through an elaborate system of funding, emanating initially from the federal government's National Endowment for the Arts, each state has an arts council that provides some funds for cultural affairs in the schools. Film rental programs can often qualify under state guidelines, and interested teachers should contact their state's arts council to see if such funds are available.

Free Film Sources

If all attempts at obtaining a film rental budget fail, there are still alternatives. Most large school districts have their own film libraries. Unfortunately, many of these are overflowing with obsolete, juvenile films that are useless today. A teacher should survey such film libraries to see just how much material in them is of any use. There probably won't be any features, but perhaps there are a few decent short documentaries. Again, an enthusiastic teacher could submit some written suggestions (call them "recommendations"—it sounds more powerful) about obtaining more recent films.

Several big city and large county free library systems have film loan services. Usually these are more up to date than school board sources. New York, Philadelphia, Pittsburgh, Los Angeles, and Chicago all have excellent catalogs of the very best short films and are adding more features all the time.* The major problem with these sources is that they only lend films for 24-hour periods. Reservations for free loans of the most popular titles sometimes tie them up for months. Therefore, if you hope to use these sources, plan your curriculum carefully in advance and book films early. Under such circumstances, September is not too soon to reserve a film for May.

One additional word of advice concerning free films. Don't be taken in by film distributors' listings of free classroom movies. These are industrial or travel propaganda films designed to sell products or company images. I remember seeing an airline-sponsored film on India that made even the most destitute sections of Calcutta look like Shangri-la. Avoid such films like the plague.

Take Your Students to the Movies

Even an extensive use of free films won't supply teachers with very many features. If rental money isn't available, the next best solution is to take a class to a theater to see a film that is relevant to the course of study. One of my best experiences of this kind was taking two classes of social studies-humanities students to see a theatrical showing of *Little Big*

---

*Some of the feature films now usually found free in regional libraries are *Citizen Kane, The Gold Rush, The Informer, David and Lisa, Nothing But a Man, The General,* and *King Kong.*

Man. The film was, of course, not yet available in 16mm, and it served as a timely resource in our discussions on human responsibility (the classes had just finished reading Seymour Hersh's book *My Lai 4*).

The major problem with this source—outside of the fact that there is less and less acceptable contemporary film fare each year—is that the admission price must come out of students' pockets. Check to see if theaters will grant a student discount or if the school will contribute to the admission cost. If the theater is a "revival house," specializing in older films, you might arrange a special rate with the manager for a slow night—Monday and Tuesday are usually poor days for theater business. Such theaters might even book films requested by teachers on such nights, if a guaranteed number of student patrons can be enough to give the owner a small profit. When I was in the classroom full-time, several of my colleagues and I made arrangements with a neighborhood theater owner for such screenings.

I realize that I have not offered here any earth-shattering solutions to the film-finding problem, but I hope I've pointed out that although the situation is difficult, it is not hopeless. There are ways of finding film sources. So persevere, and if all else fails, there's always television!

Solving the Scheduling Problem

While by no means as serious a problem as obtaining funds to run a film program, trying to squeeze even the shortest film—let alone a feature film—into the average 45-minute class period can be quite a headache. Standard interruptions (fire drills, PA announcements, hall disturbances, and the like) plus the lag time in getting the kids seated, the roll taken, the projector threaded (or repaired!), generally leaves time for about 10 or 15 minutes of screening at best. What to do?

The ideal solution is a flexible modular scheduling pattern in which teachers needing extended class time for lengthy projects, such as showing feature films, can keep a class longer by borrowing time from a colleague, who, in turn, has the same option when she or he chooses it. Many teachers are in schools where this is the norm, and scheduling a film-oriented curriculum is no problem.

My school had no such convenience. Therefore, the best solution I could come up with for showing films in their entirety was to arrange for a group of students to be block-rostered to a double period of English just before they came to my social studies class. In this way the English teacher and I used the same film and showed it in its entirety over a three-period span.

A variation of this, already practiced in many schools, is to schedule double periods of English and social studies classes one day and eliminate them the next.

What about the school that has a totally inflexible scheduling system? I realize that what I am about to suggest may offend die-hard film buffs and purists, but the simplest way to use feature films in regular period lengths is to divide them into episodes. I know that movies are artistic entities created to be viewed in one sitting, and I'm not recommending splitting films if other options are available. But if there are no other alternatives, this method can work. For example, Tony Richardson's marvelous film *The Loneliness of the Long-Distance Runner* (an excellent discussion piece on the alienation of youth) is 103 minutes long. It comes on three reels of roughly equal length. I showed it to my classes over a three-day span. Because of the film's reliance on flashbacks and its surprise ending, splitting it up can be facilitated by giving the class an assignment after each of the first two reels, such as having students predict forthcoming events. This helps sustain continuity.

Sometimes features are not divided into reels of conveniently equal length. Once I showed a film that had a 17-minute first reel, a second reel that ran slightly more than an hour, and a 30-minute third reel. To solve this problem I had to mark my place on the reels by inserting a piece of white paper at the point where I stopped, rewinding from that point. The next day I unwound the film from there and threaded my projector where I'd left my marker. The whole procedure can be very time-consuming, but it will work.

Obviously the best solution to the scheduling problem is to completely restructure the concept of the school day. The point is, however, that you can, even under the most rigid conditions, use feature films if you really want to. You can squeeze a feature film into three 45-minute periods—barring fire drills, special assemblies, principal's announcements, malfunctioning film projectors, and other natural disasters. That's better than not showing it at all.

❧ 2 ❧
Getting Started— Ten Feature Films That "Turn Kids On"

Teaching with films is a lot like teaching with works of literature. As instructors, our first job is to motivate our students, to get them interested in a subject and stimulate them to pursue it further. Just as we might select a relatively easy, colorfully written book to start a semester of literature, so should we consider this method of starting a film program in our curriculum.

No doubt many teachers have their own favorite films and have a clear idea of how to integrate them into their subject areas. However, I would like to devote this introductory chapter to an annotated list of ten feature films I have found most effective with my own students over the past few years. These films can serve a number of academic purposes in social studies and English, which are noted in each listing. The one trait they all have in common is that students *enjoy* them immensely. They are all ideal for initiating an academic program built around film.

"THE 10 THAT TURN ON"

ANIMAL FARM. 75 min., color and animated. Produced by John Halas and Joy Batchelor, Great Britain, 1955.

This marvelous animated adaptation of George Orwell's political fable is a true example of bringing a novel to life. The essence of Orwell's satirical prose is preserved in the intelligent narration and the cartoon images, particularly the evil pigs, who vividly resemble the human tyrants they represent. The only significant change the film makes from the novel is at the end, when the pigs celebrate their total control over the other animals. The book ends at this point, demonstrating the futility of revolution since the pigs have come to be exactly like the humans they replaced. In the film the animals rebel and destroy the pigs at the conclusion.

Animal Farm has great potential in English and social studies classes. It is particularly effective with slow learners and poor readers who are "hooked" by its animation.

Available from Phoenix Films for rent or long-term lease, (a black and white print is available for rent).

COOL HAND LUKE. 129 min., color. Directed by Stuart Rosenberg, 1967.

The most recent inclusion on this list, this film is already among the most popular on the classroom circuit. Paul Newman stars as a chain gang prisoner who refuses to allow his spirit to be broken by the brutality of his surroundings. The film is a complex one since the hero's nonconformity serves as an identification symbol for his fellow inmates, who vicariously fight the system through Luke's defiance, and for the film's audience, which derives similar pleasure from Paul Newman's bigger-than-life portrayal. There is even an effort on the part of the director to have the hero appear as a kind of Christ symbol. This is an ideal film for stimulating discussion on nonconformity and the nature of hero-worship.

Rental from Macmillan Audio Brandon Films, Twyman Films, or Swank Films. The complete screenplay is available in the *Identity* volume of Scholastic's "Literature of the Screen" series.

DR. STRANGELOVE OR: HOW I LEARNED TO STOP WORRYING AND LOVE THE BOMB. 93 min., black and white. Directed by Stanley Kubrick, 1964.

Cool Hand Luke

Dr. Strangelove is by far the most controversial film on this list since it brutally (and brilliantly) satirizes the American nuclear defense system. An Air Force general, appropriately named Jack D. Ripper, goes berserk and unleashes an atomic attack on the Soviet Union. A menagerie of comic opera buffoons including President Merkin Muffley, Colonel "King" Kong, General Buck Turgidson, and a sinister ex-Nazi, Dr. Strangelove, become involved in the event, and the whole thing concludes with the world coming to an end as an off-screen voice sings, "We'll meet again, who knows where, who knows when." Believe it or not, all of this black humor is very effective in provoking a serious reappraisal of American international policy.* The film is ideal for high school social studies and can be useful in English classes as a sophisticated example of social satire.

Available from Columbia Cinematheque.

THE LONELINESS OF THE LONG-DISTANCE RUNNER. 103 min., black and white. Directed by Tony Richardson, Great Britain, 1962.

---

*I should note that one slight element of this film has "dated" it in a most interesting way. The source of Jack D. Ripper's paranoia is his fear of the "conspiratorial fluoridation of water." Ripper claims fluoride in water is responsible for his impotency. With recent discoveries of the effects of additives in food, Ripper's madness doesn't seem quite as extreme as it did in 1964.

Based on the famous short story by Alan Sillitoe (who also wrote the screenplay), this film depicts the life of a working-class British teen-ager in a reformatory. Given an opportunity to represent the school in a cross-country race, the youth reflects on the meaning of his life as he runs (visualized by a number of brilliant flashbacks) and chooses in the end to deliberately lose the race rather than accept the values of the establishment. Students really identify with many of the film's situations, and I have never seen it fail to stimulate enthusiastic discussion on the nature of conformity. If the money is available, a teacher could show this and *Cool Hand Luke,* which raise many of the same questions from different perspectives. In the English class, a transmedia study analyzing the way the short story has been expanded for the screen would also be a valuable activity.

Rental from Twyman Films. The complete screenplay is available in the *Identity* volume of Scholastic's "Literature of the Screen" series.

LONELY ARE THE BRAVE. 107 min., black and white. Directed by David Miller, 1962.

The anti-establishment film is a traditional favorite among students. Keeping in mind that all the films listed here are to motivate, I especially recommend *Lonely Are the Brave,* which is in the same spirit as *Cool Hand Luke* and *Loneliness of the Long-Distance Runner.* Kirk Douglas portrays a modern cowboy who refuses to accept the depersonalization of modern society. Pursued by a mechanized posse, including a helicopter which he symbolically shoots from the sky, the cowboy represents the last stand of the "natural man." The film has an ironic surprise ending, which I have seen bring students to tears (The cowboy and his horse escape the posse only to be run down on a rain-soaked highway by a truck full of toilet fixtures). It is one of the most popular feature films I have ever used.

Rental from Universal 16 or Twyman Films.

NOTHING BUT A MAN. 92 min., black and white. Directed by Michael Roemer, 1964.

Universally acclaimed as the most honest American film about black people to date, this brilliant "little" movie is perfect for classroom studies on race relations and human rights. Its story of a black man's struggle to support his wife and maintain his dignity while living in the racist abyss of the Deep South is very moving. Although this film was made on a low budget and is not as "slick" as the others on this list, it never fails to impress audiences who see it. Ivan Dixon and Abby Lincoln are brilliant in the leading roles. It's a pity that there is no other film about blacks that even approaches the same league.

Rental from Macmillan Audio Brandon Films. The complete screenplay is available in the *Men and Women* volume of Scholastic's "Literature of the Screen" series.

ON THE WATERFRONT. 108 min., black and white. Directed by Elia Kazan, 1954.

This Oscar winner of over two decades ago has lost none of its awesome power, and today is a standard in classroom film programs. The Budd Schulberg screenplay about a young tough who acts on conscience to testify against his corrupt friends in the longshoremen's union (including his own brother) is as relevant today as ever. The realistic photography, the brilliant acting (Marlon Brando, Karl Malden, Lee J. Cobb, Rod Steiger, and Eva Marie Saint), and even the electrifying musical score by Leonard Bernstein make this one of the best of American films. I have used it in a unit on ethical problems with even the academically slowest kids. It is particularly effective with reluctant or troublesome students, who identify with many of the situations.

Rental from Contemporary Films-McGraw-Hill, Macmillan Audio Brandon Films, or Columbia Cinematheque.

PATHS OF GLORY. 86 min., black and white. Directed by Stanley Kubrick, 1957.

The film version of Humphrey Cobb's classic novel is one of the most provocative anti-war statements in screen history. Depicting a true incident during World War I, when the French General Staff ordered the execution of four innocent soldiers to serve as discipline examples against troop mutinies, *Paths of Glory* becomes a brutal condemnation of all wars. The film is cinematically excellent, including some of the most realistic combat sequences in screen history. Naturally a film like this is very emotionally stimulating, and it has motivated some of the finest, most thoughtful student essays I have ever read.

Rental from United Artists 16.

TWELVE ANGRY MEN. 95 min., black and white. Directed by Sidney Lumet, 1957.

Another classroom standard, *Twelve Angry Men* is a vivid portrayal of the operation of the American jury system. Twelve nameless men, all very average, are charged with passing judgment on an accused murderer. Although the film is highly theatrical, and perhaps a shade too contrived, the deliberation of these men in their quest for justice is exciting and informative. This film is ideal for social studies classes and might be particularly effective in junior high since it properly simplifies the judicial procedures without sacrificing the basic principles of the system for sheer melodrama. Although the whole film takes place in a jury room, director Sidney Lumet's stylistic filming keeps the situation properly tense and always entertaining.

Rental from United Artists 16.

VIVA ZAPATA. 113 min., black and white. Directed by Elia Kazan, 1952.

One class of students I taught selected this as their favorite film in a semester that featured *The Loneliness of the Long-Distance Runner, The Hill, Citizen Kane,* and *Paths of Glory.* John Steinbeck's literate screenplay (the most neglected of his works) about the rise of Emiliano Zapata, an illiterate Mexican Indian who rose to power and fame as a leader of the Mexican Revolution, is a deeply human statement of the effects of violent revolution on men. Marlon Brando's Zapata is complex and believable. This film can be used effectively in a unit on social revolution along with *Animal Farm* or it can be studied in an English class with some of Steinbeck's published works.

Rental from Films Inc. A paperback edition of the complete script is available (Viking, 1976).

❧ 3 ❧
Selected Short Subjects

Much of this book and, indeed, much of my own classroom methodology emphasize the value of full-length commercial feature films. I am, however, quite aware of the fact that the majority of teachers who use film at all use short films. Shorts—generally films that run under one hour in length—have certain obvious advantages for the classroom. They can often be shown and discussed within the context of an average class period. They are far cheaper to rent than feature films; indeed in some areas of the U.S. lucky enough to have well-endowed regional film libraries, many popular shorts can be borrowed without charge. And, unlike features, most shorts are available for purchase as well as rental, hence making them better candidates for a school's A-V center.

Yet, despite the obvious advantage of short films in the classroom, there are certain problems with them. For instance, the fact that many can be obtained free can also be a disadvantage. Often the shorts available free from libraries tend to be old television documentaries or, worse, specifically labeled "educational" films treating topics like the fall of

Carthage, the economy of modern Peru, and the asexual reproduction of frogs. Occasionally, major libraries of short films will include a few "film as art" prints, and teachers interested in more than a simple classroom visual aid will literally book and show to death classic, artistic films such as *Dream of the Wild Horses, Occurrence at Owl Creek Bridge,* and *The Hangman.* Too often classroom shorts fall into either of these two categories—dull visual aids or overshown classics.

There are currently thousands of fine, artistic, relevant, entertaining shorts in 16mm circulation that are not getting much school use. The reason for this points out another basic problem involving shorts as valuable educational tools—they cannot be readily previewed by potential users. Few theaters book shorts anymore. Television, with a handful of notable exceptions such as the CBS Children's Film Festival, rarely programs short subjects. Most short films in 16mm distribution are independently made and have little commercial value. Often the most creative shorts are experimental in their use of color, photography, editing, and the like. Many are animated. And, a large proportion of today's better shorts are foreign made, with a sizable number from Eastern Europe. The teacher who wishes to keep abreast of the availability of new titles is hard pressed to find much information beyond mere catalog listings.

Sources of Information

Here are some ways interested teachers can obtain more information about short films.

- Film catalogs. While promotional in nature, there are a few well-written distributors' catalogs which attempt to give detailed summaries and teaching suggestions. Send for the catalogs of the distributors listed in the Film Distributors Directory in the Appendices. They are free.

• Books. A number of books are currently available to teachers of screen education. *Films Deliver: Teaching Creatively with Film* (Citation Press, 1971) has a couple of excellent chapters on short films, including annotated filmographies. Pflaum/Standard Publishing Co. (Dayton, Ohio) has a useful loose-leaf guide to short films (over 100 titles) in William Kuhns' *Themes: Short Films for Discussion* (1968). It has since published Kuhns' sequel, *Themes Two* (1974) which treats 100 more recent titles. Although the new book generally lacks the specific teaching suggestions found in its predecessor, it is still a useful source.

• Film Conferences and Festivals. As a regular feature in my "Classroom Cinema" column in *Scholastic Teacher* I dealt with several of the professional teacher organizations that ran film workshops and in-service training around the country. Since that time a number of these groups have begun to wither away (largely due to lack of funds), including the parent organization, NAME—National Association of Media Educators. These groups were excellent sources for information on new films, and their decline will hurt the film study movement. If you know of a strong regional film study organization in your area (Detroit Area Film Teachers Association, for example), find out about its new films screening program.

I can recommend two, well-organized, intensive screening programs that are held each year. The Annual Midwest Film Conference meets the last weekend of each January at the Marriott Hotel in Chicago, Illinois. For more information, contact Charles Boos, c/o Viewfinders, P.O. Box 1665, Evanston, IL 60204. The American Film Festival is held annually (usually in mid-May) in New York City under the sponsorship of the Educational Film Library Association (EFLA), and while many of the films displayed are in the old-fashioned educational films mold, some of the best artistic shorts are screened as well. Interested persons should address queries to EFLA, 17 West 60th Street, New York, NY 10023, Attn: Film Festival.

Some Shorts Worthy of Note

Here, in no particular order, is a list of some potentially useful classroom shorts that are not, to my knowledge, being used as often as they should be.

60 SECOND SPOT, 25 min., color, 1974.

I have shown this relatively new film at a number of teacher workshops, and it has been a great hit. Young filmmaker Harvey Mandlin, who previously made TV commercials, takes viewers behind the scenes of the filming of a 7 Up commercial. His film deals with virtually every element of the production, from story board planning, to casting, to location filming in the Mojave Desert. The commercial—a comic spoof of British desert legion epics—is shown in its entirety at the conclusion of the film, as the whole complex, expensive process is distilled into a minute of television time. This fascinating, often funny, film is both a vivid behind-the-scenes view of movie making and a thought-provoking values lesson. Highly recommended.

Purchase or rental from Pyramid Films.

STICKY MY FINGERS, FLEET MY FEET, 23 min., color, 1972.

One of several films that was sponsored by the American Film Institute, this is the only one of that group that I have seen work with junior and senior high students. It is based on a funny *New Yorker* magazine story about a group of middle-aged, middle-class guys who play touch football in Central Park. The film is a mild spoof on sport as ritual and the macho-male self-image. It was the first effort of director John Hancock, who has since made one of the best feature films about sports—*Bang the Drum Slowly*. One slight problem with *Sticky My Fingers* is that it is about five minutes too long, and this makes some of its slow-motion football

Time-Life Films

Sticky My Fingers, Fleet My Feet

footage a little pretentious. Still, it would be a good film to use with a unit or mini-course on sports literature.

Purchase or rental from Time-Life Films.

NO. 00173, 8 min., color, 1969.

A Polish film about the future and a great discussion piece, this film portrays a bleak society in which workers literally worship their machines. A lovely red, animated butterfly causes the workers to momentarily become humanized, but with ultimately tragic results. The blending of live action and animation is artful, and the film would be a superb companion piece to the works of Huxley and Orwell.

Purchase or rental from Contemporary Films-McGraw-Hill.

LES ESCARGOTS, 10 min., color, 1968.

An award-winning French animated film that is both a spoof and an example of the horror-science fiction genre. A farmer upsets the ecological balance when he discovers that shedding his own tears on his crops causes the plants to grow to enormous size. Soon some snails begin to eat the plants, and they grow into gigantic monsters that go on a rampage. This film is sometimes funny and is a great example of artful animation. It would work particularly well in a science fiction unit. The film contains a couple of seminude drawings and thus would be best used with mature students.

Purchase or rental from Contemporary Films-McGraw-Hill.

THE IMMIGRANT EXPERIENCE: THE LONG JOURNEY, 28 min., color, 1972.

This is perhaps the best specifically made-for-the-classroom film I've ever seen. It is a realistic and humane dramatization of the life of a Polish immigrant boy and his family coping in a New York ghetto at the turn of the century.

Purchase or rental from Learning Corporation of America.

THE DOVE, 15 min., black and white, 1968.

This very funny spoof of Ingmar Bergman's films gets a lot of play in colleges, but I haven't heard much about secondary schools making use of it. The film uses fake Swedish dialogue, with riotous subtitles, and brilliantly satirical imitations of Bergman's somber imagery. Since it starts seriously, the audience is at first reluctant to laugh, though the film gradually becomes sidesplittingly hilarious. This would be a very good film for a satire unit.

Purchase or rental from Pyramid Films.

The National Film Board of Canada—A Very Special Source for Shorts

The National Film Board of Canada (henceforth referred to as NFBC) was founded in 1939 under an act of Parliament by the noted critic and documentary filmmaker, John Grierson. The NFBC's initial function was "to make films in the Canadian national interest." Although it had all of the trappings of a government-sponsored propaganda machine, the Film Board has evolved into one of the most creative producers in the cinematic world. Since the 1950s, when its aims were clarified "to interpret Canada to Canadians and to the world," the NFBC has become an international supplier of quality motion pictures.

Although technically speaking all NFBC products are supposed to have Canadian subject matter, the films have a much broader appeal. For English and social studies classes, as well as more specialized courses in film and communications, there are three basic genres of films available from NFBC.

The first of these genres or categories I call, "Film As Art ... Plus." This consists of highly creative use of the cinema medium, through techniques like animation, time-lapse photography, slow motion, freeze framing, and color, to convey some "social" message. For example, in an eight-minute film called *Toys,* children are shown gazing in a toy shop window at plastic soldiers and armaments. Gradually the mood changes from idyllic to violent. The toys seem to come to life. They engage in a battle and destroy each other. All of this is done through some superb special effects. *Toys* uses film as art to convey a humane message.

The second genre of NFBC films is a series of social "mini-dramas." These are dramatized shorts (each about 30 minutes long), using actors to deal with a particular social issue or problem. Subjects such as premarital pregnancy, dating, automation, and alcoholism are handled with all the professional skill one would expect from a good commercial feature film. Virtually all these "mini-dramas" are open-ended, providing unlimited opportunities for classroom discussion. One other element of this genre that should not be overlooked is their timelessness. They do not date. The actors are dressed in clothing that doesn't frequently change style. The cars used are Volkswagens. Hence, even though some of these films were made in the early sixties, kids will not be conscious of that fact.

The third genre of NFBC shorts is social documentaries. These documentaries have the same high production value as American television news specials but often differ stylistically. The Canadian documentaries rarely rely on an omniscient narrator. Skillful editing and location sound recording generally make up the narrative. If a narrator is used, he is most likely a participant in the events portrayed, recounting them for the viewer.

Another interesting development in the NFBC documentary film is a special series called "Challenge for Change." This is a series of films made about severe social problems in Canadian society. These films present the points of view of the have-nots of society—blacks, Indians, welfare recipients, and the aged. Often the films are made by the people themselves.

Before I recommend individual titles that worked best in my classes from each of the above categories, I should say a bit more about acquiring the films. The first step should be to obtain a free catalog by writing to:

The National Film Board of Canada
1251 Avenue of the Americas, 16th floor
New York, New York 10020

Next read through it, noting the individual distributors of films for rental or purchase; the Film Board never rents and rarely sells its prints directly. Before renting, however, first check local libraries to see if the films can be obtained free. Because of the low purchase rates, many libraries buy NFBC films.

Some Personal NFBC Recommendations

"Film As Art . . . Plus"

MULTIPLE MAN, 16 min., color, 1968.

A beautiful film using split screen images (sometimes as many as eight at a time) to show the cultural development of man. Originally shown in the Canadian Man and His World exhibit.

Purchase and rental from Contemporary Films-McGraw-Hill.

NEIGHBORS, 9 min., color, 1952.

NFBC has produced all of the films of the great animator Norman McLaren, and this is one of the best known. By animating two actors (a technique called pixillation) McLaren creates a parable about two neighbors who "war" over a flower. Winner of an Oscar in 1952 and still a powerful discussion piece.

Purchase and rental from International Film Bureau.

THE STREET, 10 min., color, 1977.

A beautifully animated excerpt of Canadian-Jewish writer Mordecai Richler's autobiography. A young boy witnesses his family's reactions to his dying grandmother. In spite of the serious subject matter, the tone of the film is gentle and often funny, since the situation is from the child's point of view. (He wants the old woman's room so he won't have to share with his sister anymore.) Ultimately he is touched by the death and begins to grow up. The film features marvelous watercolor and ink animation by Carolyn Leaf; the script is by Richler himself.

Purchase from NFBC. (To date no rental available.)

EVOLUTION, 10 min., color, 1970.

A comic, animated look at Darwin's theory. Winner of several international awards.

Purchase and rental from Learning Corporation of America.

TOYS, 8 min., color, 1967. See description above.

Purchase and rental from Contemporary Films-McGraw-Hill.

"Mini-Dramas"

PHOEBE: STORY OF A PREMARITAL PREGNANCY, 28 min., black and white, 1966.

An honest, realistic drama about a teen-age girl's pregnancy. The film ends unresolved, leaving the class with an ideal opportunity for discussing this delicate problem.

Purchase and rental from Contemporary Films-McGraw-Hill.

A MATTER OF SURVIVAL, 26 min., color, 1971.

A vivid dramatization of the impact of computers on white collar workers. I have used this film very effectively in economics units dealing with the problems of automation.

Purchase or rental from Contemporary Films-McGraw-Hill.

THE GAME, 27 min., black and white, 1968.

This is one of the very few candid, no-punches-pulled classroom sources on teen-age sexual behavior. The film deals with an adolescent boy's attempt to "make" a girl in his class and about the peer pressures and double standards of teen-age (and adult) society.

Purchase or rental from Contemporary Films-Mc-Graw-Hill.

"Documentaries"

CIRCLE OF THE SUN, 30 min., color, 1966.

An excellent film about the generation gap among modern Indians. Told from the point of view of a young Blood Indian who can neither adjust to the white world nor live on the reservation with his own people.

Purchase or rental from Contemporary Films-McGraw-Hill.

ALINSKY WENT TO WAR, 57 min., black and white, 1967.

One of the few filmed accounts of the career of the late Saul Alinsky, professional organizer of poor. This film candidly depicts Alinsky's work with American blacks. (NFBC also has two films on Alinsky's relationship with Canadian poor and the Rama Indians.) Part of the "Challenge for Change" series.

Purchase or rental from Contemporary Films-McGraw-Hill.

SAD SONG OF YELLOW SKIN, 58 min., color, 1969.

Award-winning documentary about daily life in war-torn Saigon. This film is a vivid, at times depressing, view of the impact of war on men. It also represents an expanded dimension in NFBC's production policy.

Purchase or rental from Films Inc.

Extracts of Feature Films.

Recently Learning Corporation of America has released two series of thematic excerpts from some fine feature films. Each episode had been cut to under 30 minutes in length. The first of these series, "Searching for Values," includes shorts based on such films as *On the Waterfront, I Never Sang for*

My Father, Five Easy Pieces, and *The Bridge on the River Kwai.* Each short has a particular theme and treats a basic values conflict for students to resolve. For instance, the *On the Waterfront* excerpt is entitled "Whether to Tell the Truth." These films work within the limited context of stimulating discussion, and their length is convenient for classroom screening. But film fans will object to the way they have been cut (several key shots are removed from within memorable scenes), and my own preference would be to try and show the entire feature. Still, for many teachers the series is proving to be extremely valuable.

The other LCA series is entitled "Great Themes in Literature" and consists of excerpts of other features such as *Lord Jim, In Cold Blood,* and *The Taming of the Shrew.* The scenes in these extracts are more intact that those in "Searching for Values"; indeed the material taken from a poor feature film like the Taylor-Burton *Taming of the Shrew* is actually more enjoyable as a short. However, these films are marred by some very pretentious on-screen narration by Orson Wells, who provides some "universal" literary concepts everyone could do without. Use these films as decent visual aids for literature. Period.

I should note that teachers can expect more feature film extracting programs from other distributors in the future. Even though I have personally worked on one of these, I am undecided as yet on their value in the classroom.

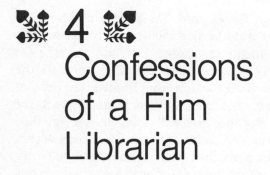

4

Confessions of a Film Librarian

During my tenure as Films Editor of *Scholastic Teacher* and in the various professional workshops I have conducted around the country, the question that I've been asked most often is how feature films can be purchased by individual schools. These queries have come from classroom teachers and school librarians who apparently have the financial wherewithal to actually buy movies for schoolwide use. Assuming large cash outlays for film libraries were beyond the means of many schools, my major concern has always been advising people how to scrape up the funds for rentals. The idea of individual schools maintaining their own film resources and media centers intrigues me however, since during my last four years as a full-time teacher I was under the impression that my school was unique in actually owning its own films.

The only way I can advise readers on the matter of purchasing films is to cite my own experience as custodian of a film library, which taught me a great deal about the educational use and abuse of the movie medium.

In the fall of 1968, the school I was teaching at was awarded a $10,000 grant from a businessmen's coalition to develop motivational programs. One of these programs included the creation of a permanent film library, and $4,000 was earmarked for the project. When I was appointed project chairman, I nearly went into shock. I had fulfilled the dream of every film teacher—enough money to run an effective program (for a year or two!).

After organizing a screening committee of interested teachers, I began ordering dozens of prints for preview for possible purchase. It was at this point that I became aware of the first major problem in creating a film library: feature films, generally, are not for sale. Legal rights of producers, movie studios, and distributors usually prohibit individual ownership of theatrical films. Therefore, my committee had to settle on a number of short films, setting aside a portion of the budget for film rental (as usual). When films are for sale, they are substantially cheaper in the long run than if rented. One short we purchased—the marvelous Czech-animated allegory on power, *The Hand*—rented for $25 per showing. The sale price, which is, of course, for unlimited usage, was only $245 (now it's considerably higher). Clearly, if a school had the money, it seemed that purchasing films was quite economical—at least this is what I believed in 1968.

My committee worked for almost three months screening the best films available. In the end we settled on 14 titles, including a seven-year lease on the feature *Animal Farm*. Our library included social documentaries from Indiana University—NET Film Service (*Where Is Prejudice?* and *The Poor Pay More*), artistic and experimental shorts from Contemporary Films-McGraw-Hill (*The Hand, Timepiece, The Hangman*), and some timely popular television documentaries (notably segments of CBS's "Of Black America" series). It was a fine, if limited, library, and we set aside enough money for feature rentals for a full school year. The committee dissolved itself, and the Simon Gratz High School film library officially opened.

As soon as the films became available to the faculty, major problems began to develop. Since I believe these problems are common to all schools with film libraries, I'll telescope four years of frustrations into a list of the basic dilemmas I had to face as custodian of the celluloid resources.

- Most teachers cannot operate standard 16mm projectors. At first this meant that they were reluctant to use the films, since many were too proud (or something) to admit their technical ineptitude. Or, they simply gave the projection responsibilities to students who claimed, or thought, they knew how to run a projector. This resulted, almost immediately, in wholesale damaging of the new films—particularly torn sound sprockets, which are irreparable and caused by faulty threading. In the spring of 1969 we had to close the library temporarily and run a special in-service program on five Saturday mornings to train teachers how to use equipment correctly. We had to deduct money from our rental budget to pay the teachers in the program for their overtime work.

- The drain on funds for teacher training left us without sufficient money to buy replacement footage for damaged films. That meant that shredded frames had to be cut out of prints entirely, and key scenes were spliced together with important dialogue or visuals missing. As of this writing, all but two of the films in the library have been "retired," damaged so badly that they cannot be threaded into machines. As for the teacher in-service program, faculty turnover has undermined that. Of the 25 teachers originally trained in 1969, only a handful remain. Hence the technical ineptness of teachers kept perpetuating itself. (The state of Pennsylvania not long ago dropped its requirement for teachers to take standard A-V courses.) I should add that new, so-called self-threading projectors are not yet perfected to eliminate these problems. Such projectors can, like teachers, automatically split films down the middle.

- A high school film library has some curricular disadvantages. Since the same films are available for all teachers, subjects, and grade levels, kids end up seeing them from tenth to twelfth grade, often two or three times a semester. One of our most popular titles, *The Poor Pay More*, was used by social studies, English, commerce, and home ec teachers. I remember showing it to a senior class in consumer problems where a student complained she'd seen it six times since tenth grade, including once in her hygiene class! (For some reason *Animal Farm* was also popular in the hygiene class and in several industrial arts classes as well.)

- Probably the biggest problem I faced in maintaining the film library was just plain teacher abuse of the movie medium. Despite a great deal of lip serve to hip terms such as "visual literacy" and "hot media," many of my colleagues looked upon film as a good voice saver. This lack of respect for the academic legitimacy of the medium and for kids led several of my fellow teachers to use the school's films to substitute their own lack of preparation. For example, teacher X walked in on Friday morning:

"Is *Animal Farm* available today?"

"No," I replied.

"How about *The Poor Pay More?*"

"No," again.

"Well give me anything. They had a test yesterday, and I promised them a movie. Besides, I have to record grades today, and while the film is on. . . ."

The presence of that cabinet full of films, unfortunately, gave too many mediocre teachers a chance to ruin a potentially effective teaching medium. As I've tried to point out often in my career as a screen educator, teachers can't show movies to kids in a vacuum. They'll know you're faking, and they'll disregard what's on the screen. Teaching with films requires creative planning, just like teaching with anything else.

Because of the problems I've listed here, I honestly cannot recommend that a school create its own film library unless its faculty has been thoroughly trained in the technology and philosophy of effective film teaching. Once this training is completed, a school could possibly benefit (and save quite a bit of money) from a film library of its own.

If your school has the funds to build its own film library, why not earmark part of the money for a special rental relationship with a single film distributor. Although few leading distributors of feature films publicize it, many of them can make arrangements with schools for block rentals of a group of features for one lump sum. For instance, a school can offer $700 to a distributor for perhaps eight or nine titles. If rented separately, these films would probably cost a lot more, but the school is offering the distributor a large account. After all, the school is in a position to divide that $700 among several companies for individual rentals. Hence, it is to a distributor's advantage to discount for a large customer.

Some major film distributors have feature film leasing policies for unlimited showings during the period leased. Such leases can be arranged so that for a lump sum a school can order one group of films for the first year, then return them and receive a completely different group the next year. This is cheaper than individual rentals, and it eliminates the problem of kids seeing the same movies each semester.

Some Film Distributors Who Sell and/or Lease

Contemporary Films-McGraw-Hill
The largest distributor of quality short films for sale, as

well as many features for sale or lease.
Pyramid Films
> Quality short films for sale or rent.

Bailey Film Associates
Carousel Films
> Both sell some of the finest television news documentaries.

Indiana University Audio-Visual Center (formerly NET Film Service)
> Sells most of the better documentaries from educational TV.

Zipporah Films
> Sells all of the noted documentaries of Frederick Wiseman.

Films Incorporated
> This is one of the largest distributors of feature films. Until quite recently, however, all that one could lease or purchase from them were shorts (and not among the best either). Today though, there are some excellent features available for long-term lease from the RKO library, which Films Inc. controls exclusively. Films available for leasing include *Citizen Kane, The Informer, King Kong, Wagonmaster,* and *Murder, My Sweet.*

Phoenix Films
> Excellent selection of short films and feature length documentaries.

Learning Corporation of America
> A superb library of fine short films and feature films from television, including *The Autobiography of Miss Jane Pitman.*

United Artists 16
> This distributor currently has long-term leases on several of the excellent features in its library, including *Moby Dick, The Miracle Worker, West Side Story,* and *Twelve Angry Men.*

💐 5 🌿
They Laughed At *Captains Courageous:* What Place Do Old Movies Have In the Classroom?

Not long ago an English teacher told me about a negative film-teaching experience. Her eighth-grade class had studied some of the works of Kipling. To enhance the unit's literary range even further, she decided to show a film of a Kipling book the class had not read. Her choice was the classic movie version of *Captains Courageous.* She realized it was an old film (1937), one she had not seen in years, but she felt her kids would accept it. They had enjoyed reading Kipling and, after all, the written works were much older than the movie. Then too, *Captains Courageous* was an award-winning film and was still heavily recommended by professional English organizations. So she saved up the rental money, motivated the class to see it, and blocked out three periods in a row to show the film at one sitting. And then she turned on the projector.

After the film was on for ten minutes total chaos erupted. The kids were laughing hysterically at the movie.

Soon their laughter turned to indignance. "Why are you showin' us this jive stuff ?"

The teacher wisely stopped the projector and began discussing the problems of the film with her class. After a few minutes she turned it on again. Out of respect for her, the class endured the rest of the film.

Interestingly enough, as the film progressed and as the kids became more tolerant of it, the teacher began to snicker. Spencer Tracy's toothy grin and fake accent, and Freddie Bartholomew's affectatious whining were silly and clichéd. The whole stilted pastiche of the MGM Atlantic bathtub looked absurdly phony. The teacher was thoroughly ashamed she'd chosen such a dated, boring old movie. She told me that she would use nothing but recent films from now on.

I fully sympathize with that teacher's predicament. It has happened to me with movies much newer than *Captains Courageous*. The only thing I can't accept is her conclusion—that only recent movies will turn students on. With over sixty years of world cinema to draw upon there are great movies—classics—that do endure for generation after generation. The teacher's problem with old films is a complex one. He or she has to know why some films can stand the test of time while others can't.

To help solve part of the problem, it is necessary to examine what "dates" movies. What are some of the specific factors that cause some films to age faster than others?

Here is a list of things I believe "date" many feature films and make them almost unwatchable in today's classrooms. This list could be used as a guide when considering an older film for students to see.

"Dating" Factors

Cinematic Style

Like any art form movies have gone through a variety of stylistic changes over the years. The old Hollywood products

RBC Films

The Great Dictator

of the 30s and 40s were made for less sophisticated audiences, hungry for illusions. Hence studio sets, stationary cameras, rear projections,* and simulated action were once enough to hold mass audience attention. Today with rapid transportation, advanced camera techniques and sound equipment, and the like, movies have moved from the confines of studios. Location filming and "realism" dominate films today (including many TV shows). Hence the limited techniques of the past tend to make many old films look stagnant by today's standards.

Many recent films are already dated by these standards. The voguish psychedelic camera techniques of the mid-60s —zoom lenses, hand-held camera, blurred focus, and other spin-offs from TV commercials—literally hit the viewer over the head with the camera. Films of this ilk are particularly annoying today. They too delete the basic illusion. They make

---

*The use of a movie screen behind the actors on which action sequences are projected creating the illusion of the actors' involvement.

viewers too conscious of behind-the-scene techniques. Take another look at *The Graduate* or *Easy Rider,* for example.

Styles of Acting

The Hollywood films of the 30s and 40s were cast from the "studio stable." Actors were under long-term contracts and generally were forced to take parts they were unsuited for. This explains the numerous examples of miscasting in older films. Spencer Tracy (whose acting rarely dates) won an Oscar for *Captains Courageous*, though the Portuguese sailor role is a clear example of miscasting.

Another example of dated casting involves the stereotypes that permeated the movies of the past. Some of these were downright vicious—particularly the roles written for blacks and Orientals. (I recall a group of twelfth graders angrily walking out on the Marx Brothers' *A Day at the Races*—a supposedly timeless comedy—because of a minstrel show sequence.) Others look absurdly clichéd—especially the

The Long Voyage Home

Films Inc.

portrayals of women and children (consider the stereotypes of Jean Harlow and Shirley Temple). Stereotypes were so prominent that many "great" films of the past require some forewarning before screening them today. (See the chapter on John Ford for some examples of this kind of "dating.")

"World View"

Motion pictures often represent the political and social attitudes of the era in which they were produced. Hence they are an excellent source of social history. However, films closely linked with attitudes of their times have little value as enduring art or as educational tools. Thus, a well-made thriller like Hitchcock's *Foreign Correspondent* (1940), while still entertaining, is essentially an anti-Nazi propaganda film. Costume epics like *Lives of a Bengal Lancer* "date" because of their embarrassing white-man's-burden attitudes. Even old westerns look absurd for their simplistic view of good versus evil and their vicious treatment of the Indian.

This is true of today's films as well. The "hip" attitudes of *Easy Rider* will look equally absurd to a future generation.

Past Folkways

All films become dated according to this criterion. The clothing, grooming, technology, and slang of the past are all preserved on film, and contemporary audiences tend to notice these factors first when seeing an old movie. However, these are the easiest elements to overcome if a film can transcend the other elements of datedness.

Really good older films are not affected much by the above factors. Somehow, despite their age, these films preserve their message for any audience. Of course, no movie 25 or 30 years old will be accepted cold by a 15-year-old kid.

He or she will giggle at the hemlines, hairstyles and baggy pants. A teacher's job, once that timeless film has been found, is to motivate the class to watch it—to build it into an appropriate unit. And, the teacher should let the class know ahead of time that the film is old and that the skirts are long (or short), and the like. Then, if the film has that enduring quality, it can speak for itself.

Author's Choice of "Old" Films for Today's Kids

After many years of film teaching I have a few personal favorite old movies that have worked well with kids. Here is a brief list of a few of them.

I AM A FUGITIVE FROM A CHAIN GANG, 90 min., black and white, 1932.

This is the oldest film on the list. This true story of a man who twice escaped the horrors of a vicious Southern chain gang has retained its powerful impact. Despite certain cinematic limitations, the film manages to look extremely good today. Paul Muni's performance was one of his greatest.

Rental from United Artists 16.

THE LONG VOYAGE HOME, 125 min., black and white, 1940.

This is one of director John Ford's least known films and one of his best. Based on four short plays by Eugene O'Neill, it is a vivid portrait of life at sea. The film is loaded with pathos and drama and would be very useful in a cross-media study examining O'Neill's plays and the screen adaptation. One cautionary note—warn your students that a very young John Wayne appears in it as sailor Ole' Olson. It is a bit difficult to endure Wayne with a Swedish accent.

Rental (of some beautifully restored prints) from Films Inc.

THE GOOD EARTH, 136 min., black and white, 1937.

This movie adaptation of the Pearl Buck classic is a classroom staple. And it deserves to be. All it needs by today's standards is color.

Rental from Films Inc.

MR. SMITH GOES TO WASHINGTON, 95 min., black and white, 1939.

Most of the films directed by Frank Capra (*Meet John Doe, State of the Union,* and so on) hold up well today. Their high idealism and good nature are rarely seen in contemporary movies, but kids react very well to them. Though *Mr. Smith. . .*isn't a very realistic look at American politics, it still stimulates a lot of valid discussion about political ethics.

Rental from MacMillan Audio Brandon Films or Twyman Films. Complete screenplay available in the *Power* volume of Scholastic's "Literature of the Screen" series.

FURY, 99 min., black and white, 1936.

Fritz Lang's thirties masterpiece was an angry indictment of mob violence. Today this film is just as impressive. I showed it one summer to a group of teen-age campers. Once they got used to the hemlines and hairstyles, they became totally absorbed. Spencer Tracy's performance as the lynch law victim who returns from the grave is beautiful.

Rental from Films Inc.

Most of the feature films of Charles Chaplin.

After many years of being out of 16mm circulation, all of the full-length films of the screen genius (actor, writer, producer, director, composer) Charlie Chaplin are now available. Some of these films are silent (*The Gold Rush, The Circus, The Kid*), others were made in the sound era but contain no dialogue (*Modern Times, City Lights*), and still others are complete talking pictures (*The Great Dictator, Limelight*). The charm, wit, and comic style of Chaplin are timeless, and these films are still incredibly funny, entertaining, and moving. I personally do not recommend *Monsieur Verdoux*—a "Bluebeard" black comedy or the limp political satire, *A King in New York.*

All these Chaplin classics are available from RBC Films. *The Gold Rush*, as well as several of Chaplin's short comedies, can also be rented from Twyman Films or Universal 16.

6
Classroom "Sleepers"

For some strange reason, which I personally cannot understand, critics have labeled certain excellent films that have had little promotional fanfare or are relatively unknown to the general public as "sleepers." (Can you imagine your students' reaction if you told them the movie they are about to see is a real "sleeper"?) Despite this rather misleading label, however, there are a number of motion pictures now in nontheatrical release that are indeed excellent and unknown to mass audiences.

Some of these films were low-budgeted, independently made pictures that could not afford major bookings. Others were critically acclaimed but, largely because of some controversial theme, failures at the box office. Still others in this category were initially poorly received by opinion-setting critical publications and were withdrawn from national distribution too soon. Whatever the cause of their obscurity, the "sleepers" listed in this chapter all have one basic factor in common—they are potentially good classroom films. They can be made to relate well to basic curriculum and, more importantly, to kids. So far, few of the films listed here are being used to such purpose as far as I know.

My opinion that these films are good educationally is based on my own experience with them. I have shown all of them to my students at one time or another, and I can attest to their relevance to the subjects I was teaching. I realize that a great many other films may meet the qualifications of "sleepers" (and there are many, many tempting catalog listings), but in order not to mislead readers, I will only recommend those with which I have had some on-the-job experience.

I've divided my list into three categories, realizing that teachers who are film aficionados will have heard of some of them. The categories are based on the amount of nationwide theatrical distribution the films had and whether or not they were shown on national television. Hence the "semi-obscure" list includes films of major studios that did have some mass distribution; "obscure" films are those that probably only appeared in major cities but were reviewed in national publications and shown on TV; and the "totally obscure" category contains films that quite possibly never got beyond art house screenings in New York and had virtually no television exposure.

Semi-Obscure "Sleepers"

THE CHARGE OF THE LIGHT BRIGADE, 130 min., color, directed by Tony Richardson, Great Britain, 1968.

No, this is not a remake of the old Errol Flynn swashbuckler nor is it a cinematic version of Tennyson's heroic poem. Director Tony Richardson (who did *Tom Jones*) has fashioned his film after the brilliant anti-war historical work, *The Reason Why*, which exposed the ineptitude of the British military of the nineteenth century. The film is an accurate account of history (using animated political cartoons to portray the passing of time) and is loaded with parallels to the military blunders and wastefulness of our own

Universal Pictures

Privilege

times—particularly Vietnam. The British cast (Trevor Howard, John Gielgud, and David Hemmings) is excellent, and I have used the film to demonstrate recent trends in historical revisionism and as a contrasting piece to the Hollywood epics glorifying cavalry charges and militarism. Its length may mean splitting up your class's screening over four or five days (if you have no way to schedule it for one sitting), but it is definitely worth the time.

Rental from United Artists 16.

HAMLET, 115 min., color, directed by Tony Richardson, Great Britain, 1969.

This most recent screen version of Shakespeare's tragedy did not do well commercially, and many will still prefer Laurence Olivier's traditional film interpretation (1950). But Nicol Williamson's portrayal of the great Dane as an angry firebrand, and some vivid cinematic technique make this a very exciting movie. I recommend showing it as part of a trans-media study with students who have read the play and/or seen the Olivier film, noting the varying interpretation in each version.

Rental from Columbia Cinematheque, or special secondary school purchase can be made from Learning Corporation of America; (The Olivier *Hamlet* can be rented from Twyman Films).

BURN, 120 min., color, directed by Gillo Pontecorvo, Italy, 1970.

A flawed but devastating film about a fictitious, early nine-teenth-century slave rebellion, which has many parallels with today's black power struggle. Made by the man who directed the brilliant and controversial *Battle of Algiers* and starring Marlon Brando as the British agent who for political reasons encouraged the rebellion and then ultimately became its suppressor, *Burn* is a powerful and relevant film. Although some insensitive editor cut out a few important sequences, hurting the film's continuity, I recommend it highly. I used it in a unit on revolution, and my students did some of their best analytical writing after screening it.

Rental from United Artists 16.

Obscure "Sleepers"

A FACE IN THE CROWD, 125 min., black and white, directed by Elia Kazan, 1957.

Elia Kazan's lost masterpiece is a movie that was truly ahead of its time. Based on a Budd Schulberg short story (he also wrote the screenplay) about a hillbilly singer who becomes a television idol and then a diabolical political force, this film brilliantly predicted the future impact of television as an image-making medium. I used it regularly in my civics courses along with Joe McGinniss' book, *The Selling of the President 1968*. The film only recently became available in 16mm (after disappearing from cir-culation for 14 years).

Rental from Charlou Films, Inc. Screenplay available in the *Power* volume of Scholastic's "Literature of the Screen" series.

WAR HUNT, 81 min., black and white, directed by Denis Sanders, 1962.

This chilling little film received some high critical acclaim in 1962 and has been shown on television. However, no one involved in film study ever seems to have heard of it. *War Hunt* is about the psychological effects of combat. A young infantryman (John Sax-on) becomes a hero by going on mission after mission in Korea, silently killing his enemy with a stiletto. When the cease-fire comes, he is upset and refuses to accept it, even to the point of sneaking out at night to kill enemy guards. To compound matters, he has adopted an eight-year-old Korean boy who has begun to emulate his foster father's behavior. This premise is truly frightening, and it raises all sorts of questions about the behavior legitimatized by war.

Rental from United Artists 16.

PRIVILEGE, 103 min., color, directed by Peter Watkins, Great Britain, 1967.

A futuristic drama about a totalitarian society that uses a rock singer to condition and harness mass opinion. Director Peter Watkins uses the same semi-documentary style in his Oscar-winning *The War Game*, and the film is a powerful 1984ish commentary. Critics were too quick to dismiss it when it was released. They should have witnessed the reactions of teen-age audiences before helping to bury it commercially. *Privilege* is ideal for a unit on power and propaganda.

Rental from Universal 16.

Totally Obscure "Sleepers"

KES, 110 min., color, directed by Ken Loach, Great Britain, 1970.

A real undiscovered gem of a movie. This realistic film about a lower-class Yorkshire teen-ager's affection for a trained kestrel falcon may sound like an animal film, but it definitely isn't. Using the boy-bird relationship to underscore the basic good nature of the youth, the film is more a portrait of growing up in a poor, English mining town. The scenes of the boy's high school are a vivid condemnation of a brutalizing educational system. The animal theme and the uncompromising use of the Yorkshire dialect, which often strains American ears, hurt the film commercially, but it should provide a great classroom experience.

Rental from United Artists 16.

THE OLIVE TREES OF JUSTICE, 90 min., black and white, directed by James Blue and Jean Pelegri, France (English subtitles), 1961.

A quiet, compassionate film about people caught in the whirlpool of revolution. Without hysterical polemic or tasteless exploitation of violence, the filmmakers present the problems of a young Algerian-born Frenchman seeking his identity in the revolutionary Algeria of the late fifties. Although the film's pace is deliberate and the subtitles might turn off students with reading problems, *The Olive Trees of Justice* can be a useful source for social science and humanities classes.

Rental from Contemporary Films-McGraw-Hill.

THE EXILES, 72 min., black and white, directed by Kent Mackenzie, 1961.

Humane films about Indians are very "in" right now, reflecting the belated guilt of filmmakers for all their stereotyping in the past. However, this excellent documentary on the efforts of three young Indians to adapt to urban life in Los Angeles has been around for a number of years, and few have noticed it. Very depressing in its graphic exposé of the evil discrimination against Indians, it should be required screening in all classes discussing minority problems. *The Exiles*, up to now, is a documentary too few educators know about.

Rental from Contemporary Films-McGraw-Hill; also available for purchase.

Kes

United Artists

7
Foreign Language Films

For a long time during my years in the classroom as a "movie teacher," I was reluctant to use foreign language films. There were a number of reasons why I hesitated to show them, and I think many other teachers may be similarly skeptical of such films. My worst problem with them was that many of my students were poor or reluctant readers. Often I used films to motivate these kids to read or as substitutes for literary works. A subtitled movie, I felt, wouldn't work very well with them. Even better readers, I found, often reacted negatively to subtitles, as do many adults. Indeed, foreign language films have been declining in popularity in the United States. Compared to the 1960s, very few subtitled films are being released here, and even fewer of these make any money. In 1973, for instance, no major American distributor would touch Ingmar Bergman's *Cries and Whispers,* and when it finally was released by an unknown company, it barely broke even financially.

In spite of this general decline of the foreign language film in America and in spite of its disadvantages in the classroom, I am becoming a strong advocate of incorporating such films in the curriculum.

First of all, *not* showing foreign films to students would be denying them the experience of some of the greatest cinematic art. No course in film study should really fail to expose viewers to the works of Bergman, Fellini, Truffaut, or Kurosawa. Traditional courses in world cultures, world literature, values and, of course, foreign languages can also benefit greatly from screening international films.

Suggested Guidelines

I have prepared a list of a variety of good foreign language films I feel most secondary students can relate well to. However, first I'd like to propose a few guidelines for showing these films.

- If your students are not used to subtitled films, try to choose ones that depend more on visual imagery and action than dialogue. Although the eye ultimately adjusts to seeing the image and reading the titles, many cinematic details can be missed by students struggling to read line after line of subtitles. Don't, for instance, choose a film as talky as Eric Rohmer's *My Night at Maude's*.

- Before you show any of these films, emphasize to students that they needn't read every subtitle to enjoy and appreciate the film. Tell them to try and watch it like any other movie, concentrating on its visual style, acting, and sound track. I have seen kids try to take notes from subtitles, fearing they are going to miss something. Discourage this.

- If reading is a problem among your students, check to see if there is an English-dubbed version of the film. Of course, dubbing is not usually very well done, and out-of-synch voices can make a serious film look humorous; but occasionally there is a decent English-language version, and for students who read poorly, this is really the only choice.

- If you are not sure how students will respond to a subtitled film, try showing a short to test their reactions before investing in a feature. I have included on the list a few short films that can be used as trial pieces. If they work well, then go ahead and invest in a feature. I especially stress this point since full-length foreign films are generally among the most expensive to rent.
- When showing a subtitled film, make sure that you can totally darken your room. Black window shades are essential, since light reflection will blur the print of the English words at the bottom of the screen.

An International Sampler of Foreign Language Films

France

LES MISTONS (The Mischief Makers), 18 min., black and white, 1957.

This delightful, bittersweet, short film by Francois Truffaut would be a perfect introduction to foreign cinema for even junior high students. A group of preteen boys mischievously follow a pretty young woman around on their bicycles and in the process, learn about the meaning of love and growing up.

Purchase or rental from Pyramid Films.

NIGHT AND FOG, 31 min., color and black and white, 1955.

Alain Resnais' famous documentary about the horrors of the Nazi concentration camps, narrated in French. This film is so full of unforgetably powerful images that students don't have to be able to read the titles to get its message. However, the narration is both poetic and extremely meaningful, and teachers using the film might want their students to discuss narration. The script is available in English in *Film Books II: Films of Peace and War,* edited by Robert Hughes (New York: Grove Press, 1962), pp. 234-55.

Purchase or rental from Contemporary Films-McGraw-Hill.

The Battle of Algiers

THE 400 BLOWS, 98 min., black and white, 1959.

Truffaut's masterpiece about a twelve-year-old's experiences in reform school is one of the foreign language films most heavily used in high schools.

Rental from Janus Films.

THE BATTLE OF ALGIERS, 123 min., black and white, 1966.

This is an Italian-produced, French-language film directed by Gillo Pontecorvo, which has been publicized as a textbook for revolutionaries. Actually, it is a superbly made, fictionalized account of a phase of the Algerian revolution. The film favors the revolutionaries but is surprisingly complex in its portrayal of the events. It is not a simple, left-wing polemic.

Rental from Macmillan Audio Brandon Films.

Italy

LA STRADA, 107 min., black and white, 1954.

Federico Fellini's classic film about the tragic relationship of three circus performers—a brutish strong man, a philosophical clown, and the pathetic, simpleminded waif, Gelsomina, who affects both of them. This film is a must in any cinematic curriculum.

Rental from Macmillan Audio Brandon Films.

THE ORGANIZER, 126 min., black and white, 1964.

This is a starkly vivid re-creation of the conditions of factory labor in late nineteenth-century Europe. It is also one of the few films that honestly treats the rise of organized unions. Marcello Mastroianni stars as the idealistic scholar who leads the workers' cause.

Rental from Twyman Films. An English-dubbed print is available upon request.

Japan

WOMAN IN THE DUNES, 123 min., black and white, 1964.

This is one of the greatest and most exhausting cinematic experiences I've ever encountered. An insect collector, stranded in a strange town, accepts temporary lodging in the house of a woman who lives at the bottom of a sandpit. When he tries to leave, he discovers that the townspeople have removed the ladder from the pit. He is thus condemned to live with the woman and forced to shovel sand for the town in return for food. This film is both a mystery and an allegory, and should prove a stimulating experience for students. The subtitles, I might add, are brief and easy to read.

Rental from Contemporary Films-McGraw-Hill.

The Seventh Seal

Janus Films

RASHOMON, 83 min., black and white, 1950.

Akira Kurosawa's masterful film has been adapted in several other versions, including a stage play and, of all things, a western movie. However, this classic tale of four interpretations of the murder of a nobleman and the rape of his wife should be seen in the original Japanese. The film will work extremely well in classes examining the concept of literary point of view.

Rental from Janus Films.

Sweden

THE SEVENTH SEAL, 96 min., black and white, 1956.

This is probably Ingmar Bergman's most popular film in secondary schools, and it deserves to be. The symbolic story of a knight who plays a chess game with the Angel of Death to forestall the black plague from wiping out a town is also the screen's most realistic re-creation of the medieval world and mind.

Rental from Janus Films. *The Seventh Seal* screenplay is available in English translation in *Four Screenplays by Ingmar Bergman* (New York: Simon & Shuster, 1965).

SHAME, 102 min., black and white, 1968.

Another masterpiece from Bergman, this film is not yet heavily used in classrooms. It too is an allegory—this time on war's effects on humankind. It depicts the degradation of a peace loving, modern man and woman whose world is shattered by a strange war in which friend and enemy are indistinguishable. Starring Max von Sydow and Liv Ullmann.

Rental from United Artists 16.

India

THE APU TRILOGY. Three films by Satyajit Ray: PANTHER PANCHALI, 112 min., black and white, 1954; APARAJITO, 108 min., black and white, 1957; THE WORLD OF APU, 103 min., black and white, 1959.

Each of these fascinating dramatic films depicts phases in the life of a Bengali family as seen through the eyes of a son, Apu. The films, seen separately or in succession, provide a memorable portrait of Indian life. These films would be superb in a world culture curriculum.

Rental of each film from Macmillan Audio Brandon Films.

Senegal

BLACK GIRL, 60 min., black and white, 1965.

One of the few African films available in the United States, *Black Girl* was written and directed by the Senegalese Ousmane Sembene. The film deals with the struggle of a young African girl trying to cope with the French colonial family she serves. Although technically imperfect, this film is a deeply moving anti-colonial statement.

Rental from New Yorker Films; apply for rate.

8

The Documentary-
As-Visual-Aid
Syndrome

The most heavily used 16mm films in secondary schools today are documentaries—particularly news and historical documentaries originally produced for network TV. The reasons for the popularity of such classroom standards as *Cities of the Future, Mark Twain's America, The Population Explosion,* and *The Real West* is not hard to figure out. Teachers see them as good instructional visual aids. Documentary films, many teachers argue, deal with real people and events—all their visual elements are actual portrayals of real life. Most documentaries are self-teaching, since they contain intelligent, informative narration from such masters of communication as Orson Welles, Chet Huntley, Howard K. Smith, and that pillar of respectability, Walter Cronkite. These films are excellent introductory motivators or concluding reinforcers to existing curriculum units, their defenders would argue. They are also, usually, the least expensive films to purchase or rent and are the most easily obtainable without cost from school district or public libraries.

While all these facts are generally true, I have to admit

that I would rather see teachers use no films at all than have them show old television documentaries as visual aids. The blind acceptance of the content of such films as "truth" betrays a serious lack of critical media sophistication on the part of teachers and students alike. For example, take one of the most popular classroom films—a piece called *The Twisted Cross*. The school I used to teach in even owned its own print of this NBC Project 20 documentary on the history of Nazi Germany.

The Twisted Cross is by no means a bad film. It is a typical compilation film, made up of old clips from World War II newsreels, German propaganda films, and other archive sources. Its detailed narration describes many of the better-known events in Hitler's rise and fall. Teachers use the film as a historical visual aid, yet there is something about its content that is unrecognized in many classrooms. The film contains quite a few brief cuts from old Hollywood movies, in addition to its newsreel and captured German footage. There is one rather extensive sequence showing families being viciously dragged from their homes by Nazi Storm Troopers, which is from a 1943 "quickie" called *Hitler's Children*. Now you could argue, "So what?" After all, the Nazis actually were this brutal, so the film isn't really lying by incorporating the fictional clip. Or is it? The narrator doesn't indicate that a different kind of source has been tapped. The screen credits at the beginning and end of the film don't cite the Hollywood movie. And the whole thing is stamped with the seal of an "NBC News Production." In an era of unprecedented saturation of television news reporting, I don't think I am overstating the case by saying that for many people, lamentably, NBC News and truth are synonymous.

There are similar problems with so-called "real-life" documentaries. These films depict behavior in present day society by focusing on contemporary incidents (school desegregation, unemployment, student protests, national security leaks, and the like) and institutions (mental hospitals, prisons, the nuclear family, and so on). Yet, they too reflect the points of view of their producers. These documentaries contain subjects specifically *selected* by their filmmakers.

The style of filming is equally selective. A close-up of a key figure in a film at a certain point is designed to elicit a particular emotional reaction on the part of viewers. Camera distances and angles are all deliberate *choices* of the filmmakers. Documentary films are, of course, deftly edited, especially those planned to fill a particular TV time slot. Hence the images viewers see are mere pieces of the entire subject the film is portraying. Again, what is seen is the choice of the filmmaker.

The order of sequences and the content of the narration (if there is one) also condition viewers' responses to a film. There have even been documented cases of falsified visual aids in such films. The most famous case of this kind was in CBS' powerful 1968 documentary *Hunger in America*. This very humane depiction of various groups of Americans who were literally starving in the late 1960s opened with the shocking sight of a deformed infant lying on a table. Charles Kuralt's narration then commenced—"This baby is about to die of prenatal malnutrition." Suddenly the camera zooms in, revealing that the baby is dead. However powerful this scene is CBS officials later admitted that the photographed infant was born prematurely and was *not* dying of malnutrition.

The point that I wish to make is that documentary films are not necessarily more true to life than acted, commercial films. Documentary films generally represent cinematic journalism. Just as teachers teach kids to deal critically with opinion versus fact in print, so too must we teach them to make similar distinctions in the electronic media. Using TV documentaries as straight "factual" classroom visual aids only contributes to the problems of "media illiteracy."

Now that I've made my case against the general use of documentary films in the classroom, I would like to present a different educational approach to this type of film. I believe that documentary filmmaking can be among the most exciting and creative of cinematic arts. I really want documentaries to be incorporated into the school curriculum—not as visual aids but as journalistic and artistic filmed essays. To approach documentaries in this way, I offer teachers the following guidelines that recognize the need to emphasize the subjectivity of such films as the first priority. I have also included a sample list of a few documentary films which can be treated as a self-contained unit in visual literacy.

Guidelines for Teaching with Documentary Films

1. Begin by showing any standard TV news documentary or assign one on prime time television. Ask students to write a paragraph or two summarizing its content. Then briefly discuss the film's basic theme and message in class.
2. After students have analyzed the surface content of the documentary, ask them to try to recall the *way* this material was presented. Ask some of the following questions:

    - Did the narrator's words always match the visual images? Were there any scenes which you would have liked the narrator to describe further? Which ones? Why?
    - How was music used on the film's sound track? What particular scene do you recall where the musical score enhanced its excitement?
    - Which people in the film did you like most? Which did you like least? Why? Which people in the film do you feel you knew most about? Why?
    - Do you believe the material you saw portrayed on film was true? Why, or why not?

3. If possible, show the film again. Ask students to reconsider their previous judgments in light of the film's structure. Alert them to how the film was edited (which scenes follow and precede each other, and what they add up to), when extreme close-ups or distorted camera angles are used, and what elements of the material do not seem fully developed.

4. Have students create, either in an essay or through a visual storyboard, an altered version of the film. Have them re-edit the various scenes into a different order, changing the meaning and message of the film. This activity will help students to see that "real" characters can easily be made into "actors" through the filmmaking process.

5. Introduce students to the work of an artistic documentary filmmaker who is conscious that he is not simply reporting facts. There are many superb contemporary documentarians—Arthur Barron (*Sixteen in Webster Groves, Birth and Death, Factory*), Fred Wiseman (*High School, Hospital, Law and Order*), the Maysles brothers (*Gimme Shelter, Salesman*)—whose work can be sampled to illustrate this type of film as a creative essay.

After screening one of these films, have students undertake the same kind of structural analysis they applied to the TV film.

In conclusion, let me emphasize that documentary films can be vital classroom tools if students are encouraged to approach them for what they are—creative, subjective essays in celluloid.

Some Recommended "Creative" Documentaries
MAN OF ARAN, 77 min., black and white, 1934.

A must in any unit on the documentary is one of the classic films of American Robert Flaherty. This particular film portrays

Man of Aran

the harsh everyday existence of the people on an isolated island off the coast of Ireland. The film is both realistic and poetic (especially because of its lush musical score) and is an example of documentary art at its best.

Rental from Contemporary Films-McGraw-Hill.

THE PLOW THAT BROKE THE PLAINS, 21 min., black and white, 1936.

During the Depression, the United States government commissioned filmmaker Pare Lorentz to depict the causes of the dust bowl erosion of the Great Plains. The film was designed to boost the government's new policies of agrarian reform. The result was considered a haunting, vivid documentary in its day—a great example of advocacy screen journalism. Today it comes across as slightly corny.

Rental from the Museum of Modern Art, Macmillan Audio Brandon Films, and available free from many regional libraries.

THE MARCH OF TIME SERIES, numerous episodes about 20 min. each, produced from 1935-1949.

This famous series of "news" shorts exemplifies the potential dishonesty of the documentary genre. Heavy narration, stirring music, staged sequences, and the personal philosophy of Time-Life's Henry Luce were the forte of these films. Use them to show early negative trends in documentary news reporting.

A few original episodes are available from Time-Life Films.

HARVEST OF SHAME, 58 min., black and white, 1961.

One of the greatest of all TV news documentaries, this CBS "See It Now" film (produced and narrated by Edward R. Murrow) exposed the horrible working conditions of migrant laborers. The film is an example of cinematic muckraking at its best.

Rental from Contemporary Films-McGraw-Hill.

HIGH SCHOOL, 75 min., black and white, 1969.

Frederick Wiseman's brilliant film essay about the dehumanizing nature of an affluent, white high school is almost an indictment of the entire American educational system. This film clearly represents the attitudes of its maker and presents many opportunities for critical analysis depending on the predisposition of its viewers.

Rental from Zipporah Films; apply for secondary school rate.

ESSAY ON LONELINESS, 22 min., black and white and color, 1970.

One of the most creative, moving documentaries I have ever seen. Arthur Barron depicts moments in the lives of several New Yorkers which emphasize the film's basic theme of loneliness. It includes several unforgettable sequences, including one of a woman's face as she undergoes an abortion. The film is truly what it says—a subjective essay on the human condition.

Currently not available.

MONDO CANE, 102 min., color, 1963.

One of the all-time commercial successes (next to *Woodstock*) and an absolute cinematic mess. Italian exposé journalist Gualtiero Jacopetti created his hodgepodge of weird customs around the world in an effort to show that Europeans and Americans are as savage as any of the primitives in the South Seas or Africa. This piece of fakery, with its staged and heavily "arranged" sequences is an excellent starting point for teaching students about potential trickery in the name of documentary "facts."

Rental from Macmillan Audio Brandon Films.

9
Obscenity
Is a
Four-Letter
Word

For the most part I have tried in this book to provide a rational—if perhaps a bit overly optimistic—case for the value of movies in the classroom. The quality films of the past, and even the sociologically interesting genre "junk" I have recommended, are valuable, and generally untapped, academic tools for teachers. However, I'd be less than honest if I didn't deal with a very real problem that has begun to confront film teachers and that threatens the very existence of screen education.

This problem is not lack of funds or lack of administrative support for school film programs; rather the problem is caused by the contemporary movie industry itself and the new levels of vulgarity it has descended to in recent years. Hollywood is caught in a terrible moral muddle stemming from recent social and political trends. All the evidence is that this muddle will result in a new low in movie quality, culminating in slick, superficial, increasingly violent films with virtually no classroom value whatsoever.

This problem can be best explained by examining the

71

four stages of its development over the past decade or so, and how each of these affects teachers who wish to show, or even recommend, contemporary films to their students.

Growth of Pornography

The first stage of this dilemma began in the late 60s with public bookings of previously underground pornographic films, and it is still prevalent to a great extent. As a result of the huge financial failures of overblown musicals (efforts to copy the success of *The Sound of Music* with such films as *Dr. Doolittle, Hello Dolly, Star,* and *Finnian's Rainbow*) and war epics (*Longest Day* spinoffs, including such duds as *Battle of the Bulge, Tora! Tora! Tora!,* and *Kelly's Heroes*) during the 1960s, most Hollywood studios began to cut back on production in fear of bankruptcy. This austerity move created huge voids in theatrical bookings. The Supreme Court early in that decade had ruled that nothing could be obscene if it had "redeeming social value." Thus the void in movie production was soon filled by "cheapie" producers (Russ Meyer, for example) who made low-budget sex films, which would be difficult to label obscene. Later the big studios began producing more sexually liberal films (20th Century Fox even hired Meyer!), and many, like their grade B counterparts, made some easy profits. The next step was the gradual release of hard-core sex epics (the earlier films simulated sexual relationships, whereas later *nothing* was left to the imagination). It is sad but probably accurate to say that historians analyzing the popular culture of the early 70s may well describe the period as the *Deep Throat* era.

Despite the fact that there were some very high quality sexually explicit films of the late 60s and early to mid-70s (*Midnight Cowboy, Last Tango in Paris, A Clockwork Orange, Dog Day Afternoon*), it was the excess that caused the trouble. Suddenly there was public indignation against such films. Police, politicians, clergy, and other citizens decried the licentiousness of these movies, though to this day hard-core pornography continues to earn enormous profits. It is interesting to note that since irate citizens have not been able to stop pornographic movies, they've begun focusing their hostilities on areas where they *can* exercise control—particularly schools. Such groups have succeeded in creating fierce censorship battles over text materials. Militant community anti-intellectualism on such matters stems, in part, from the collective frustration of not being able to control the destiny of one's own community. I don't think it's a coincidence that when parents were storming the board of education in Charleston, West Virginia, in the fall of 1974, threatening to burn literature anthologies, that in downtown Charleston most of the movie houses were showing hard-core porn.

Rating System

This leads me to the second stage of the problem with today's films—the Motion Picture Production Association's rating system (MPAA). This system, which has been in effect since late 1968, was designed to advise parents on the kinds of films they could take their children to see. (The current ratings are G—general audience, no restrictions; PG—parental guidance advised, the film may have material unsuitable for preteen-agers; R—admission restricted to those over age 18, unless accompanied by a parent or adult guardian; and X—admission restricted to those over 18—and in some communities 21.) The system is the movie industry's own, it is purely voluntary, and it is considered a reasonable alternative to censorship. Clearly with the trends in filmmaking today, some kind of advanced warning on subject matter is necessary for discriminating audiences, and the ratings do serve that purpose.

What then, is wrong? First of all, the ratings have

become far more flexible since their inception in 1968. As films have become more daring the ratings have become more lenient. Hence a film that received an R back in 1969, would quite probably be a PG film today. The MPAA still seems to use "prolonged" frontal nudity and certain four-letter words as bases for an R rating. Its judgments have been liberalized about other, less explicit profanity, quick snatches of nudity, "suggested" sex, and most of all, violence. A film can be highly adult in theme, containing all of these factors, and it will probably get a PG. Examples include *Papillon* (1974) and Sam Peckenpah's *The Killer Elite* (1975)—horrifying blood-baths children could go to see without parental approval (only "parental guidance").

Perhaps the best example of the rating system's failure concerns the R given to *The Exorcist* (1974). This hideously depraved (and extremely popular) movie featured incredibly sickening special effects, unbelievable profanity (uttered by a child, or at least a voice dubbed over a child's mouth), and suggested scenes of disgusting sexual abuse. The chief of the rating board, Jack Valenti, argued that the film deserved the R since "nothing was overtly shown." Of course his "nothing" means no nudity or sexual relations. He did not mean violence and profanity. I guess I'm particularly upset about the film not being rated X—"no children under 17 allowed"—because the night I saw it several children were in the audience, including a few four- to six-year olds whose parents brought them to see it for a "religious" experience. (In case you don't know, the movie is about some priests trying to drive out the devil.) A film like this could cause young children great psychological harm, since all of its horrors are splattered all over the screen for over two hours. Kids that young (and older) have no idea what a movie is—to them it's reality—and the rating board, by allowing easy accessibility to *The Exorcist*, has demonstrated that violence is supposed to be less offensive than sex.

There is another thing wrong with the ratings that I'm sure the MPAA never originally anticipated. Filmmakers today have used the ratings as an unusual rationale for the movies they make.

A Hollywood studio official once told me: "The PG is the best rating to get. People consider G films kids' pictures, so we try our best to spice scripts up enough to make them adult." In other words, I must assume, movies that might be made without some suggested sex and profane language, now "throw them in" just to be labeled "adult" enough.

Generally speaking, I think this studio official was right on target. The ratings not only advise adults what kids can see, they tell them what they can see as well. And today, I suppose, expectations for adult content are different from what they were ten years ago. (If you following this rationale, films like *Citizen Kane, Treasure of Sierra Madre, Some Like It Hot,* and *On the Waterfront* would all be G rated today. Does that make them children's pictures? What would be added to "spice" them up with to get a PG?)

Lack of Censoring Criteria

This leads me to the third stage of the problem with today's movies and the one that depresses me the most. As a result of public outrage against pornography (books and magazines as well as films) a number of lawsuits have been filed in federal courts by local communities against accused smut peddlers. On June 21, 1973, the U.S. Supreme Court (containing four Nixon appointees, and thus considerably different philosophically from the bench of the 60s) ruled in a 5 to 4 decision that individual states and their local communities could set their own standards for what is obscene and what is not. Chief Justice Burger further commented that a determination of what is "prurient" or "patently offensive" should be made locally on the basis of "how the average person, applying contemporary community standards, would react."

Although the surface of this decision seems most democratic, it has begun to mean the creation of some very arbitrary standards of censorship around the country. As I pointed out earlier, the thrust of community instituted censorship hasn't really hurt the movie industry at all. Hollywood has been able to successfully counter the relative handful of picture bannings since the Court decision with carefully and expensively prepared legal defenses. Hence, the center of community censorship has become public education. This is affecting the kinds of literature teachers teach as well as the films they want to show their students.

A teacher friend of mine in the Midwest was told by his department chairman not to show the 1972 film *Walkabout* (which I had recommended a number a times in my *Scholastic Teacher* column and at film conferences), because, in spite of its PG rating, the film's snatches of nudity might give reactionary members of the local community some ammunition under the Court ruling. I assume this will also mean, in some areas of the country, that teachers will have to be extra careful about even what films they recommend students see.

Sensational But Safe

The fourth stage of the problem with today's movies is the direct result of what I have discussed so far. Today Hollywood is deliberately turning out movies designed to be "safe" under the current legal guidelines and yet sensational enough to satisfy the public's apparent taste for cheap thrills. (The current flourishing porn trend is not coming from the legitimate film industry.) Both the ratings board and the Supreme Court have reacted primarily to overt sex on the screen. As I've tried to indicate, other offensive materials, particularly violence, is not considered much of a problem. Hence a movie like *The Exorcist* is safe by almost all standards. And, we are bound to see more films like it during the next few years.

Another safe genre of films is male-male love stories. While these films are not homosexual (at least not overtly), they deal with male comradeship and attitudes. Women are merely sexual decorations or ego outlets for the male heroes. These films are usually violent ("action is OK in a man's flick"). They are also causing a furor among actresses who are finding it tough to get parts in movies because of this trend. Such films—*Scarecrow, The Sting* (at least this one is not violent), *Papillon, The Super Cops, California Split, Thunderbolt and Lightfoot, Deliverance, Sorcerer, The Killer Elite. . .* the list seems endless—are almost all rated PG, and I haven't read of one being busted for obscenity by some local community. Most of these movies have been great box office successes.

Maybe the best way today's films can be treated in the classroom would be in the form of values lessons. Teachers might discuss with students just what our society means by obscenity; and then, what it *should* mean. Indeed, the legal background summarized in this chapter and the cinematic examples cited might provide a basis for such a unit.

2

Making Films Work:
Some Strategies
for the Classroom

❧ 10 ❧
The Cross-Media Message: Teaching Literature with Film

Traditionally, the greatest users of 16 mm films in the classroom are English teachers. Part of the reason for this is the relative flexibility of the secondary language arts curriculum. Phase electives, mini-courses, and thematic units abound, particularly in grades ten to twelve. If a school offers a film course (film appreciation or filmmaking), it is generally found in the English department. The heaviest consumers of feature films are literature teachers. A personal survey of my own among some leading film distributors reveals that the largest chunk of their school market (below college) is based on movie versions of novels. *To Kill a Mockingbird, The Grapes of Wrath, Fahrenheit 451, Oliver Twist,* and *The Heart Is a Lonely Hunter,* for instance, are all films that seem to be very popular among junior and senior high school English teachers.

Two Common Classroom Uses

It's not hard to guess how these films are being utilized in the curriculum. A movie is generally used in one of two basic ways. First, a teacher wants to motivate his or her students to read a particular piece of literature. An exciting film adaptation, while not necessarily faithful to the entire printed text, might, and generally does, make an interesting literary appetite whetter. This approach is obviously very successful. Nowadays movie companies are constantly working with paperback publishers to provide new editions of novels on which current films are based. (Warner Brothers, for instance, was responsible for getting Thackeray's *Barry Lyndon* into its first American printing in over 100 years as a promotional tie-in to Stanley Kubrick's movie of that book.) Or, and this practice is even more common, movie companies sponsor writers to do novelizations of original filmscripts, which then sell very well on paperback book stalls. Hence, we can thank Hollywood moguls for such paperback best sellers as *French Connection II, The Great Waldo Pepper,* and a novelization, not the original Kipling story, of the script of *The Man Who Would Be King.*

In spite of my slight cynicism about using film as literary motivation, I should emphasize that the approach does seem to work.

The second way films are most often used by literature teachers is as "reading reinforcement." This involves screening the movie version of a story, novel, or play after the class has finished reading it. Some teachers may use a film as a kind of treat or reward for the class for having struggled through the printed work. Others use a film to clarify the content to students—which is a pretty good idea if the movie is a reasonable translation of the text. I've most often seen this approach work well with films of Shakespeare's plays.

Again, I have no complaint with teachers who approach film in this way. For me the only problem is that it limits the teaching capacity of the film medium. It is my hope that English teachers might have some broader goals for film and literature study than simple motivation and reinforcement.

Teachers who wish to use film in the above mentioned ways miss one fundamental fact about the motion picture form. Great works of literature—stories, poems, novels, plays—almost never translate well on the screen. In a brilliant and very witty article in the *New York Times* (April 20, 1975) author Anthony Burgess argued that the best movies are almost always based on pop literature, works of little psychological depth or philosophical content. *The Godfather, Rosemary's Baby, Gone with the Wind,* and *Rebecca* were all masterful film versions of novels—indeed probably better than their literary counterparts. As for efforts to film great literary works—*Ulysses, The Great Gatsby, War and Peace*—Burgess' advice to movie makers is "forget it."

Basically I agree with Burgess. A teacher trying to deal with *The Brothers Karamazov, Lord Jim,* or *Huckleberry Finn* should be advised to stay away from their movie counterparts (in *Huck Finn's* case all three versions). Even for motivational purposes such films prove almost totally inadequate.

The Cross-Media Approach—and Beyond

For me, the best approach to the study of literary films has been cross-media, or transmedia, analysis. Basically this involves a detailed comparison of the similarities and differences between a printed work of literature and its cinematic counterpart. How much of the original format of the book, story, or play was preserved on the screen? How did the filmmaker substitute visual language for text narrative? Were characters and plot seriously altered in the screen version? Why would a filmmaker want to make such alterations? Is the film version necessarily inferior to the literary work, if such changes are made?

The strength of this kind of cross-media approach is that it gives students a chance to appreciate the differences between print and film—the strengths and weakness and the unique characteristics of each as a narrative medium.* It is also a good way to teach literature in general, since it involves students in a very detailed study of an author's style as well as the structure and form of the story, novel, and play. A classic such as *Moby Dick* might prove very difficult to teach in an average high school literature class today. Melville's complex style—the shifting from almost scientific descriptions of sea life to vivid dialogue interactions to biblical prose—however brilliant, mystified readers even in his own time. Yet the timeless theme of that novel deserves to be taught, and students who read it and then examine John Houston's and Ray Bradbury's streamlined film content can consider the various alternative possibilities the novel offers to script adapters. Indeed, this is what I consider the greatest ultimate value of the cross-media approach—turning students into script writers.

One of the most difficult things to teach in an English class is creative writing. Our goal as teachers is to get students to write correctly—grammar, punctuation, and sentence and paragraph structure must all be emphasized. Yet at the same time, we want to involve them in the creative communication of ideas. Noted English educators such as James Moffatt (in *Towards a Student-Centered Language Arts Curriculum*) and Alan Purves (*How Porcupines Make Love*) have indicated that scripting and dramatizing are among the best approaches to creative writing. By engaging students in a cross-media literature-film study, a teacher can provide a built-in lesson in creative scripting. The screenwriter and director have been charged with transferring a printed narrative to a new, more visual format. After students have examined several screen adaptations of literature and assessed the suc-

---

*For an excellent analysis of the differences between print and film in this instance see Charles Suhor's "The Film/Literature Comparison," *Media and Methods*, December 1975, pp. 56-9.

cesses and failures of these works, they can undertake their own scripting based on other works of literature. For instance, a teacher can have a class read Ambrose Bierce's story *An Occurrence at Owl Creek Bridge* and then screen Robert Enrico's short, no dialogue film version. After the students have engaged in a thorough cross-media analysis of story and film, they can read another Bierce story, perhaps "The Mocking Bird" or "Killed at Resaca," and try to write their own screen versions, substituting visual symbols, sound effects, dialogue, and the like for the author's omniscient narrative. With longer stories, novels, or plays students can be assigned to script individual scenes. This type of assignment might work well if a class is divided into small groups, with each group tackling a different segment of a literary work.*

To me cross-media study in an English class is perhaps the best demonstration of the film medium as a true extension of the language arts curriculum.

A Highly Selective List
of Films for Cross-Media Study

Short Stories

AN OCCURRENCE AT OWL CREEK BRIDGE, 27 min., black and white, France, 1962.

French filmmaker Robert Enrico's version of Ambrose Bierce's story has become a classroom classic. The portrayal of the momentary hallucinations of a Civil War soldier awaiting the gallows is positively brilliant. However, I almost hesitate to mention it since it is almost shown to death by teachers who have access to it. Yet it represents one of the finest examples of cinematic translations of literature. I also recommend Enrico's film of Bierce's *Chicamauga* as well.

---

*This activity would probably work better if students could see samples of actual movie shooting scripts. Many of these are published each year by leading paperback publishers.

Both films are available for rental or purchase from Contemporary Films-McGraw-Hill; also available for free loan from many regional film libraries.

JUST LATHER, THAT'S ALL, 21 min., color, 1975.

A beautiful suspense film based on a little known short story by Hector Tellez. An apparently meek barber is secretly a member of an underground revolutionary movement. When the villainous captain of the government's forces enters his shop for a shave, the barber suddenly finds himself in the position of potential executioner. Will he cut his enemy's throat?

Purchase or rental from Learning Corporation of America.

THE ROCKING HORSE WINNER, 91 min., black and white, 1950.

My own favorite cross-media film, this feature takes the eerie D.H. Lawrence story about a boy who picks winning race horses by riding his rocking horse, and transfers it into an incredibly moving tale of the loss of love between a child and his parents. All the characters are enriched by the screenplay, and the film is a virtual textbook on skillful story to movie adaptation.

Rental from Janus Films. (A 28-minute, color version is also available, but despite its professional production values, it is too literal to be much more than an audio-visual aid. Purchase or rental from Learning Corporation of America.)

THE BIRDS, 100 min., color, 1962.

Alfred Hitchcock's stunning science fiction film of a Daphne du Maurier story about birds wreaking vengeance on mankind. Du Maurier's stories translate well onto the screen. I was also very impressed with Nicholas Roeg's film of her longer story, "Don't Look Now," a diabolical tale about a couple haunted by the ghost of their child. This film might be difficult to use in a classroom, however, since it contains a nude love scene, which got it an MPAA R rating.

Rental of *The Birds* from Universal 16 Films, Twyman Films, or Swank Films; rental of *Don't Look Now* from Films Inc.

O. HENRY'S FULL HOUSE, 117 min., black and white, 1952.

While O. Henry's stories hardly qualify as great literature, their punchy plots and touches of irony have always made them

great fun in the classroom. This film consists of five of his best tales: "The Cop and the Anthem," "The Ransom of Red Chief," "The Last Leaf," "The Clarion Call," and "The Gift of the Magi." There is an all-star cast including Charles Laughton, Marilyn Monroe, Richard Widmark, and John Steinbeck as the on-screen narrator.
Rental from Films Inc.

I should add that there has been a screen attempt at Ernest Hemingway's autobiographical "Nick Adams Stories," called *Adventures of a Young Man*. Unlike the O. Henry film, which is simply an anthology of five stories, *Adventures*. . . tries to weave the stories together into a narrative. The results are monumentally unsuccessful, especially in the casting of a nonentity named Richard Beymer as Adams (Hemingway). There is, however, one episode in the film worth noting and seeing. It is Hemingway's story "The Battler" about an encounter between Nick and a punch-drunk ex-boxer at a hobo jungle campfire. Paul Newman gives a mesmerizing portrayal of the boxer, and the vignette comes as close to pure Hemingway on the screen as I have ever seen.
Rental from Films Inc.

THE AMERICAN SHORT STORY: A FILM SERIES, 1977.
A major development in the fiction-to-film genre, this series of nine 25-40 minute films based on short stories by major American writers was a critical and popular success on public television in 1977. Made possible by a grant from the National Endowment for the Humanities, the series is particularly noteworthy for its solid production values (each film is in color and reflects a fairly substantial production budget), its professional acting performances (by stars such as Irene Worth, Ron Howard, Shelly Duval, LeVar Burton, John Houseman), and the scripting and directorial work of several major film makers (Arthur Barron, Joan Micklin Silver, John Korty, Jan Kadar). The individual films themselves, however, vary in quality, largely because some of the stories they are based on were probably inappropriate for filming in the first place. This is particularly true of the version's of Hemingway's *Soldier's Home* and Ambrose Bierce's *Parker Adderson, Philosopher,* which are interior monologues. The best films in the series, it seems to me, are those that stem from literature that is mostly surface narrative

with standard plot lines and simply drawn characters. F. Scott Fitzgerald's frivolous little magazine story, *Bernice Bobs Her Hair*, emerges as the series' most entertaining film, and the versions of strong narrative tales such as Sherwood Anderson's *I'm a Fool* and Stephen Crane's *The Blue Hotel* will probably work best in a classroom situation. Other titles in the series are: *Almos' a Man* by Richard Wright, *The Music School* by John Updike, *The Jolly Corner* by Henry James, and *The Displaced Person* by Flannery O'Conner.

The total series or individual episodes are available for purchase or rental from Perspective Films.

Novellas and Novels

THE INNOCENTS, 92 min., black and white (cinemascope only), 1960.

A stunning film of the Henry James novella *The Turn of the Screw*, adapted by Truman Capote. In this version (there are others), the governess who sees ghosts ruling the lives of her children is portrayed as a sex-starved old eccentric who just may be hallucinating (though viewers never know for sure).

Rental from Films Inc.

MOBY DICK, 116 min., color, 1956.

An excellent screen distillation of Melville's novel, marred only by the serious miscasting of a wooden Gregory Peck as Ahab.

Rental from United Artists 16.

EAST OF EDEN, 115 min., color, 1955.

Writer Paul Osborne and director Elia Kazan took a pompous, overwritten Steinbeck novel (full of pretentious biblical allegories) and literally chopped out two-thirds of its content. The result is a splendid, brilliantly acted film about a young man's struggle to choose between good and evil. The book is mostly about Adam Trask, a powerful moralistic rancher, and his wayward wife who deserted him and their two sons, Cal and Aaron (Caine and Able). The movie focuses on the sons, particularly Cal, played by the legendary James Dean in his screen debut. This film would be excellent for a cross-media study, since it is a clear example of how a film can be superior to the novel.

Rental from Twyman Films, Macmillan Audio Brandon Films, and Swank Films.

ELMER GANTRY, 145 min., color, 1960.

Director-writer Richard Brooks has often been drawn to works of literature for his films. Generally he has failed (*Lord Jim, The Brothers Karamazov*), but with this uneven novel of Sinclair Lewis about a bogus evangelist, he succeeded admirably. Burt Lancaster won an Oscar in the title role and has been playing it ever since.

Rental from United Artists 16.

GREAT EXPECTATIONS, 115 min., black and white, 1947.

This British film, with John Mills, Alec Guinness, and Jean Simmons, is still the best screen adaptation of all of Dickens' works for me. It is very true to the book, yet it has a lovely narrative elegance of its own. The early scene of Pip's confrontation with the

Romeo & Juliet

Films Inc.

convict in the marsh is a masterful example of skillful editing for suspense. Directed by David Lean.

Rental from Janus Films.

MR. ROBERTS, 123 min., color, 1955.

Believing as I do in Anthony Burgess' assumption that great literature almost never makes great film, I cite the rather trivial collection of World War II navy stories by Thomas Heggan as perfect movie material. Actually the stories were first adapted into a highly successful play, but the *Mr. Roberts* film represents the beginning of a new genre—the anarchic service comedy, the grandfather of MASH.

Rental from Macmillan Audio Brandon Films, Twyman Films, or Swank Films.

ROSEMARY'S BABY, 136 min., color, 1968.

This pop novel was transformed into a movie (near) masterpiece. Roman Polanski has taken the chilling idea behind Ira Levin's book about a girl impregnated by Satan and turned it into a low-key tour de force horror film. It's a pity that the adapters of a more interesting book of Levin's, *The Stepford Wives,* couldn't turn it into much of a movie.

Rental of *Rosemary's Baby* from Films Inc.

Plays

HENRY V, 137 min., color, 1945.

Laurence Olivier's famous version of the Shakespearian history play begins in the Elizabethan setting of the Globe Theater and then miraculously opens up into a cinematic spectacle of medieval England. The Battle of Agincourt sequence is especially fine.

Rental from Twyman Films. (Note: I similarly recommend the Olivier versions of *Hamlet* and *Richard III*, both also available from Twyman Films.)

ROMEO AND JULIET, 129 min., color, 1968.

This is the Franco Zeffirelli version, and the only one I recommend. Here is a film about the ill-fated lovers, using most of Shakespeare's text but emphasizing outdoor locations and physical action. There is nothing stagebound about it. (There is a similar, totally cinematic version of *Macbeth*, adapted and directed by Roman Polanski. I hesitate to recommend it, however, since it is extremely violent and has an R rating.)

Rental of *Romeo and Juliet* from Films Inc. Rental of Polanski's *Macbeth* from Columbia Cinematheque.

THE MIRACLE WORKER, 107 min., black and white, 1962.

William Gibson's play has become standard reading in high schools, and since few productions of it are performed anymore, the only way most students will get to see it is through this excellent screen adaptation. Director Arthur Penn has used a number of complex cinematic techniques—especially in dealing with Annie Sullivan's reminiscences about her own childhood—which lift it from the stage. It is interesting to note that this play had its origin on live television.

Rental from United Artists 16.

A VIEW FROM THE BRIDGE, 110 min., black and white, 1962.

For some reason most of Arthur Miller's plays have not translated well onto the screen, but this film of his effort at a modern Greek tragedy is very good. The location filming on the New York waterfront gives the drama a realistic dimension.

Rental from Twyman Films.

THE EFFECT OF THE GAMMA RAYS ON THE MAN-IN-THE-MOON MARIGOLDS, 98 min., color, 1973.

There are a lot of flaws in this Paul Zindel play about an insensitive mother's relationship with her two adolescent daughters, but screenwriter Alvin Sargent and director Paul Newman have completely restructured it as a film. If viewers did not know *Marigolds* was originally a play, they would probably never know it by looking at the film. This is a masterful job of re-creating a story for a different medium.

Rental from Films Inc.

11

The 20th Century on Film: A Course in United States Contemporary Social and Political History

History teachers, take note! What I am about to propose is a new, more dynamic approach to those standard units on 20th century America. More and more academic historians have begun to rely on so-called popular culture sources in analyzing the past. Works such as Henry Nash Smith's *Virgin Land* and John William Ward's *Jackson: Symbol for an Age* examine the political and social events of the 19th century through songs and ballads, popular novels (including even the most risqué), oral traditions, and even graffiti. The results have been some of the most vivid, interesting, and readable pieces of historical study now available. Teachers who use materials like these and who search for similar data might try looking at the motion pictures of the last 60 or so years as the kind of social reflectors that can provide the vivid images of the past students need to grasp the significance of history.

The course of study I have outlined here is merely a suggestion. The topical groupings can be rearranged more chronologically. The number of films per unit should suit both a teacher's time schedule and budget. Actually the films listed are those I've used with classes of high school eleventh graders over about five months of the school year. I have also used these films and others in my college course, "The Film As American Social and Intellectual History," at the Center for Understanding Media.

As you read the proposed outline, keep these considerations in mind:

- All the films cited are portraits of the times and societies in which they were produced. Hence they are not audio-visual aids (as a teacher might, say, use *Ivanhoe* to teach the Middle Ages—as if that was what *Ivanhoe* portrayed!), but actual historical sources.

- Several of the films are *not* works of cinematic art (though a few are) and standard movies-as-curricula guides don't usually apply. They, therefore, have the advantage of being in little demand and consequently rent for very low rates. This means even the skimpiest budgets can accommodate them.

- The films should be used to portray the political and social events they both depict and are a part of. I am certainly not recommending them as the only sources in the unit. Teachers should still keep their standard texts or whatever supplementary readings they would normally use with their classes.

Topics and Films

Course Introduction

Some historical events were recorded on film in the era when the motion picture camera was considered an exotic toy. They are all, of course, in black and white.

FILM SOURCE: NEWSREEL, 1895-1915.

A 22-minute reel of clips of events including the Klondike Gold Rush (1898), San Francisco Earthquake (1906), and the sinking of the Austrian Battleship, *St. Stephen* (1915). This can serve as an introduction to the use of the film medium as a recorder of events.

Rental from the Museum of Modern Art at a very low rate. If a teacher wishes further use of this source, the Museum has other newsreel compilations as well.

THE MARCH OF TIME series (1935-1948), demonstrate a subjective film treatment analysis of news events. These are also available at a fairly low rental rate. Time-Life Films, Inc. also has some of these editorialized documentaries. However, Time-Life has taken these episodes and pieced them together as so-called "factual" documentaries of contemporary history, and in the process the series lost its flavor as an artifact and became primarily a visual aid. For studies like those suggested here, I only recommend using the original complete episodes of *The March of Time*, not the edited versions.

Rental from Time-Life Films, Inc.

The Film Makes History

During the latter part of the so-called Progressive Era, the administration of Woodrow Wilson faced a national issue raised by the cinematically brilliant, yet violently anti-black film, *The Birth of a Nation*. Its creator, D.W. Griffith, pioneered many modern editing and camera techniques while depicting a slanted, biased view of Reconstruction in the post-Civil War South. The villains of the film are blacks (actually white actors in blackface) and evil Northern carpetbaggers. The heroes are the Ku Klux Klan. This film was soundly condemned by the infant NAACP in 1915 but, nevertheless, praised by President Wilson and the majority of white Americans who saw it. *Birth of a Nation* is in part responsible for the creation of the modern KKK, which paraded in public down Washington, D.C.'s Pennsylvania

Avenue in 1919. The film, therefore, should be shown in class and analyzed for its viciously effective content.

It can be rented from the Museum of Modern Art or Macmillan Audio Brandon Films (print is silent). I have published a student anthology text—*The Black Man on Film* (New York: Hayden Book Co., 1975) which includes many contemporary writings about the film, pro and con. However, teachers seeking a specific single source for student reading could obtain an article by Thomas Cripps called "The Reaction of the Negro to the Film *The Birth of a Nation,*" published in Bobbs Merrill Reprint Series.

The Film As Political Propaganda

This is the first topical unit that cuts across chronological lines. Here a teacher can show one or a few significant films designed as propaganda for a particular political cause. Here are a few suggestions.

OCTOBER 10 DAYS THAT SHOOK THE WORLD, silent, 1927.

Sergei M. Eisenstein's Soviet-sponsored celebration of the Lenin Revolution. Cinematically brilliant but (obviously) very slanted. It is like a broad political cartoon, depicting how the early Soviet regime saw itself.

There is a special 60-minute version of this available from Macmillan Audio Brandon Films, which I recommend for high schools. The full 107-minute version is also available from Macmillan Audio Brandon and the Museum of Modern Art.

TRIUMPH OF THE WILL, 1936.

Leni Riefenstal's famous Nazi propaganda film depicting the Nuremberg pageants of 1934 did much to "sell" Hitler to the German people. The film is devastatingly powerful (and frightening).

Again, a short version (40 minutes) is available from the Museum of Modern Art. The full two-hour print can be rented from the Museum, Macmillan Audio Brandon, or Contemporary Films-McGraw-Hill. Though the film is in German, with very few English titles, its visual power will still come across to students.

MISSION TO MOSCOW, 1943.

An American feature made specifically to "warm up" public opinion toward an approaching detente with Russia during World War II. The film glosses over the terror of the Stalinist regime and presents the Russians as lovable, gruff people. Based on the writings of former U.S. Ambassador to Russia, Joseph E. Davies, the film, nevertheless, represents a government-sanctioned piece of propaganda, Hollywood-style.

Rental from United Artists 16 Films.

BIG JIM McCLAIN, 1952.

A terrible movie, made by and starring John Wayne, designed as a song of praise to the McCarthyists of the early fifties. Though the film is cinematically dull, it is a vivid representation of the right-wing official American hard line of that era.

Rental from Warner Brothers Film Gallery.

The Film As War Propaganda

This unit deals specifically with efforts of the American film industry to unify the public during war time. Unfortunately, the one memorable World War I propaganda film, D.W. Griffith's *Hearts of the World,* has temporarily been withdrawn from 16mm circulation. Therefore, most suggestions deal with the Second World War Era.

FOREIGN CORRESPONDENT, 1940 or CONFESSIONS OF A NAZI SPY, 1939.

Both are examples of commercial movies intended to stimulate anti-Nazi feelings in the then isolationist United States. Both films were well received and influential in their times.

Foreign Correspondent is available from many local film exchanges at very low rental rates. *Confessions. . .* rents from United Artists 16.

THE RAMPARTS WE WATCH, 1940.

This was a *March of Time* feature-length semi-documentary designed to alarm America of Nazi aggression and encourage preparedness. Though the film looks awkward today, it had impact

in its day (particularly enraging isolationists). It includes a sequence from a frightening Nazi propaganda film called *Baptism of Fire*.
Rental from Macmillan Audio Brandon Films.

BATAAN, 1943.

One of the earliest and most powerful Hollywood glorifications of American fighting men, the film creates a microcosm of America in a small patrol (Irish, Jew, Chicano, Pole, "country boy," "city boy," etc.) doomed to die in their defense of a Philippine outpost. This sort of story once had great national appeal.
Rental from Films Inc.

THE GREEN BERETS, 1968.

The only recent example of a pro-war propaganda film, John Wayne's simpleminded epic was very popular during its initial release, despite protests against it. The film is useful for discussion, analyzing the parallels Wayne and his followers see between World War II and Vietnam, especially since *Green Berets* is a World War II film in modern dress.
Rental from Macmillan Audio Brandon Films, Twyman Films, or Swank Films.

Film Views an Epoch of History—The Depression

More films were produced during the 1930s than in any other decade. Some of these reflected the Depression era realistically; others were designed as pure escapism (films of this type usually were about millionaires). This list includes well-known titles that can easily be applied to a study of the period in the classroom.

Realistic Portrayals

DEAD END, 110 min., black and white, 1937.

A film of the famous Sidney Kingsley drama, adapted by Lillian Hellman, depicts slum conditions in New York in which a group of youths worship a gangster. The film is stagy but loaded with depression philosophy. Directed by William Wyler.
Rental from Films Inc.

THE GRAPES OF WRATH, 115 min., black and white, 1940.

John Ford's film of the Steinbeck novel about Oakies in California requires no comment.

Rental from Films Inc.

THE PLOW THAT BROKE THE PLAINS, 21 min., black and white, 1936.

Pare Lorentz's slightly pretentious but moving short documentary on the Midwestern dust bowls of the mid-thirties.

Rental from the Museum of Modern Art.

Escapist Films

IF I HAD A MILLION, 73 min., 1933.

An all-star Paramount movie in which a rich man leaves a million dollars to several unexpecting benefactors. Typical of the "rich man" films of the times, its moral was, "Money isn't everything." The film was used to promote banks and restore confidence in them after the bank holiday of 1933.

Rental from Universal 16.

THE GOLD DIGGERS OF 1933, 98 min., 1933.

A typical Busby Berkeley musical of the depression, including

Dead End

Twyman Films

songs such as "We're in the Money" and a sensational torch song ballet finale called "Remember the Forgotten Man," portraying with sympathy all those who had to turn to relief and bread lines. Rental from United Artists 16.

This course could go on almost indefinitely. Teachers can use films to depict issues such as pacifism (*All Quiet on the Western Front*), stereotypes (*The Green Pastures*), imperialism (*Gunga Din*), and "whitewashed" U.S. History (*Union Pacific, In Old Chicago, Tennessee Johnson*). Other chapters in this book demonstrate some additional opportunities for this approach. Teachers who adopt this approach may be on the verge of revitalizing the history curriculum, and that would be quite an accomplishment!

12
Doin' the Fifties—
"Yeah, Yeah, Yeah"

"Rock Around the Clock" and "Mona Lisa" were on the Hit
Parade . . . Uncle Miltie was a household word . . . people
held each other while dancing . . . the D.A. was a hairstyle . . .
and everybody liked Ike. Those were the days of the 1950s . . .
filled with innocence and the promise of even better days to
come.

So read the promotion for a popular TV series called
Happy Days. The show opens with a shot of a typical drive-
in, pre-McDonald's "burger haven." The sound track blares
a scratchy version of Bill Haley and the Comets doing "Rock
Around the Clock." Thanks to the time machine of television, viewers are supposed to be transformed back to the
golden days of their adolescence in their blissful, not-so-inno-
cent, innocent years. The 28 to 35 generation has finally come
of age. Now we have a nostalgia all our own.

The media saturation of fifties nostalgia is a fascinating
phenomenon. Besides the *Happy Days* program (a real insult
to most viewers' intelligence, I might add), we are bombarded

with TV commercials, magazine ads, movies, and even "put-on" Rock groups that shout the same message—youth had a great ol' time back in the 1950s. One of the early 70s best motion pictures for me was *American Graffiti,* which brilliantly presented the decline of that era (actually the film took place in 1962), though it too contained a sentimental core implying that somehow the fifties were better times than now.

This preoccupation with nostalgia—particularly the sentimentalized fifties—would make an ideal subject for an English or social studies unit or mini-course. Such a unit should address itself to questions such as: What is nostalgia? Does each generation look back on a particular era and romanticize it? What may there be about our times—what dilemmas, frustrations—that makes recollection of the past so inviting? What kind of a decade was the fifties? Was it really a time of innocence; was it indeed a better time than today? Are there any direct cultural links between the fifties and the present? Have the fifties influenced the current life-style? In twenty years will this current decade be recalled with similar nostalgia?

Cinematic Background

Throughout this book I've indicated that a good way to examine the values and attitudes of the past is to view some motion pictures of the era being studied. Many films of the fifties provide valid reflections of the social, intellectual, and political environment of the decade, and when screened in proper context, they can tell students much about those times.

Before setting up a few potential classroom units, I should add some introductory data for teachers. First of all, not every film produced from 1950 to 1959 would be suitable for this kind of study. During the fifties many excellent movies were produced which simply do not date, and hence would be of little value in such a unit. *Sunset Boulevard* (1950), *Singin' in the Rain* (1952), *On the Waterfront* (1954), *Bridge on the River Kwai* (1957), *Some Like It Hot* (1959), and similar examples of cinematic excellence are simply not appropriate for a unit like this. The films a teacher should seek out are those which *specifically* reflect their times—in other words, movies that are "dated."

Two excellent books on film history a teacher might find valuable as background reading for this study are Charles Higham's *Hollywood at Sunset* (Saturday Review Press, 1972) and Andrew Dowdy's *Movies Are Better Than Ever* (Morrow, 1973). Both books deal with the movie industry and the tremendous changes affecting it during the fifties. Television as a popular home medium had destroyed a major part of the movie market, and major studios were forced to curtail budgets, make fewer films, and, in some cases, shut down altogether. Federal antitrust suits brought an end (at least temporarily) to the studios' ownership of theater chains. This forced an economic crisis in the movie industry and radically changed the pattern of national film distribution. Forces like these caused Hollywood in the fifties to become gimmick conscious. 3D, Cinemascope, Vista Vision, and Cinerama were all innovations designed to prove that, "Movies are better than ever" (or at least, better than television).

In addition to the economic crises threatening the film industry, a severe political storm was brewing as a direct spin-off of the Congressional anti-Communist purges of the early fifties. The specter of McCarthyism haunted Hollywood in those days. Hundreds of writers, directors, and actors were blacklisted for alleged Communist sympathies; ten were even sent to jail.* The movies became, perhaps reluctantly, a

---

*A superb, if not quite objective, book for classroom study on this subject is Eric Bentley's documentary play *Are You Now or Have You Ever Been?* (Harper, 1972) with word-for-word actual dialogue from the HUAC Hollywood hearings.

showcase for right-wing politics until the later years of the decade.

The social history of the movie industry during the fifties is almost crucial to any unit studying films of that decade. Even such typical, bland, trivial, and overblown cinematic productions as *The Robe* (1953), *How to Marry a Millionaire* (1955), *Strategic Air Command* (1956) reflect the rigid conformity of an industry under great economic and political pressure.

Once teachers have gained some insight and background on the films of the period, they can begin one of several possible approaches to a study of the fifties in the classroom. The start of any unit on the fifties should focus on what the primary attraction that era has for people today. It might be a good idea to have students watch a rerun of *Happy Days* on TV (in spite of its inane scripts and production values) as an example of the fifties craze in the seventies. A contrast to this is the brutally funny song by composer-singer David Amram called "The Fabulous 50s," from his *Subway Nights* album (RCA), which exposes the fifties as a repressive, apathetic, and boring era, not worthy of any of the current nostalgic fuss. This record raises all sorts of issues about *why* the fifties may look so good in retrospect and what that tells us about our own times.

Comparing the 50s and the 70s

After the background has been set and students have a rationale for the study, it might be a good idea to examine the cultural ties between the fifties and seventies. There are two strong, visible links between the decades that students should be aware of—rock music and youth culture. The fifties have traditionally been classified as the original rock n'roll decade, and the music of that period is highly influential on the rock music of the seventies. Indeed, some of the biggest musical promotional successes ever have been rock revival shows on

TV, in the movies (particularly documentary films such as *Let the Good Times Roll*), and on concert stages around the country featuring fifties recording stars like Little Anthony and the Imperials, Freddy Cannon, and Chubby Checker. Rock music, which had its roots in black rhythm and blues sounds of even earlier times, is a dominant cultural influence, and it had its popular origin in the fifties. Students already know this, and thanks to the perennial nostalgia of most Top 40 radio stations, the music of the fifties is as alive as ever.

The fifties, with its "new music" was also responsible for the beginning of a new preoccupation with youth. The baby boom of World War II had spawned a nation of teen-agers by 1955, and the mass media of the decade began to portray and glamorize the adolescent. Dozens of youth movies and TV shows were created, and a few of these became legendary. Most of the films portrayed teen-agers as rebellious and highly individualistic. Not only did these kids have their own music and style of dress, they had their own distinct life-style. Gone were the stereotypes of Henry Aldrich, Archie, and Junior Miss. The fifties were the era of Brando and James Dean. To a large extent, with a difference in grooming and clothing styles, the tough youth image of the fifties has been sustained through the seventies.

A class examining cultural ties of the two decades could look at one or all of the following films to find existing parallels:

THE BLACKBOARD JUNGLE, 101 min., black and white, 1955.

Maybe the most famous youth movie until *Easy Rider,* this adaptation of Evan Hunter's sensationalistic novel about a teacher in a tough urban school introduced a whole set of new teen-age types, paving the way for such epics on delinquency as *Rebel Without a Cause, Dino, Crime in the Streets,* and even *West Side Story.* "Jungle kids" such as Sidney Poitier, Vic Morrow, and Raphael Campos were a far cry from the "lovable" Dead End Kids, or the Gas House Gang. The film is also notable for its opening

musical sound track—the original "Rock Around the Clock."
Rental from Films Inc.

REBEL WITHOUT A CAUSE, 111 min., color, 1955.

The young method actor, James Dean, became the quintessential fifties teen-ager in this touching film about affluent delinquents groping for identity. Dean made only three movies before his untimely death in an auto accident, and his role in *Rebel* became the source of a cult worship for years after his death. Watching this film, which is *very* dated, is like looking at ghosts of some distant, alien, long-gone civilization. For today's kids it can be a textbook on the fifties.

Rental from Macmillan Audio Brandon Films, Twyman Films, or Swank Films.

ROCK PRETTY BABY, 94 min., black and white, 1956.

One of the dozens of cheaply made rock musicals of the mid-fifties, which used a loosely plotted teen romance as the background for lots of loud sounds of the times.

Rental from Universal 16.

Rebel Without A Cause

Twyman Films

THE GIRL CAN'T HELP IT, 96 min., color, 1956.

A very funny spoof of the fifties rock phenomenon, though its message for adults of that decade was, "It'll never last!" The film also contains some sensational examples of early artists like Little Richard and Gene Vincent, and it co-stars Jayne Mansfield, one of the many imitations of the decade's prototype glamour girl, Marilyn Monroe.

Rental from Films Inc.

Influence of Early TV on Film

Another classroom approach to a study of the fifties—particularly for an English or communications course—would be to examine the influence of the infant TV medium on film. In addition to studying the economic upheavals in the film industry caused by television, students should become aware that by the mid-fifties the movies were relying more and more on TV for fresh talent and material.

Virtually all the new faces in the films of the fifties—Paul Newman, James Dean, Joanne Woodward, Charlton Heston, and Rod Steiger—had been participants in the "golden age" of live TV drama. Programs such as Armstrong Circle Theater, Studio One, Philco and Goodyear Playhouse, Kraft Television Theater, The U.S. Steel Hour, and Playhouse 90 provided the airwaves with live, sixty- to ninety-minute drama every night of the week. By 1954 the movies had stopped trying to compete with television and began to incorporate it. In addition to building a new stable of film stars from TV, Hollywood began hiring the writers (Paddy Chayefsky, George Axelrod, Rod Serling, Reginald Rose, Tad Mosel), and directors (Sidney Lumet, John Frankenheimer, Arthur Penn, George Roy Hill) who had been responsible for the public's desertion of the movie houses for the home sets. The result of this cross-media fertilization was a series of once highly regarded, somewhat pseudo-realistic films, which reflect the popular taste of the fifties. Here are a few examples for possible classroom screening:

MARTY, 91 min., black and white, 1955.

This was perhaps the most famous screen adaptation of a TV play, winning an Oscar in 1955. The plot—a fortyish Italian-American butcher falls in love with a homely old maid—was the antithesis of standard Hollywood romance and seemed to represent a kind of revolution in romantic film prototypes. Today it looks, at best, quaint, and the once-considered realistic dialogue sounds pretentious. Still students should see it as an example of a popular cultural creation of its times.

Rental from United Artists 16.

PATTERNS, 86 min., black and white, 1956.

The late Rod Serling's writing had been a staple of video drama well into the seventies, though in recent years he had tended to be less heavy-handed and pompous than in his "prime" in the fifties. The Serling drama once consisted of a lot of heavily breathing people making profound speeches, all leading to some kind of climactic revelation. There was so much of this kind of drama in the fifties that students should look at some sample of what people once considered profound stuff. *Patterns,* about a generation gap among big business executives, is a typical example of fifties middlebrow.

Rental from United Artists 16.

NO TIME FOR SERGEANTS, 111 min., black and white, 1958.

A typical service comedy, which probably influenced the Gomer Pyle syndrome, this film was based on one of the fifties' most popular and critically acclaimed TV plays. It also became a very popular stage play.

Rental from Twyman Films or Swank Films.

TWELVE ANGRY MEN, 95 min., black and white, 1957.

This is probably the best film to emerge from the golden age of TV, and it is one of the few good films about the American jury system. Still, it has the look and tone of a film of its decade—a kind of inoffensive liberalism prevails as the good guy juror is able to win over the other eleven members who represent a very obvious cross

United Artists

Marty

section of American life. It would be interesting to ask students how this kind of film might be made today.

Rental from United Artists 16.

Influence of Right-Wing Politics

Still another approach to the fifties might be to examine the impact of right-wing politics on the films of the decade. There were a limited number of specific anti-Communist films made early in the decade, though, for the most part, Hollywood just dusted off old spy melodramas to illustrate the Russian menace. Plots of old World War II espionage epics were revised, substituting Soviets for Nazis and Japanese. Another more subtle approach was through a series of alien invasion science fiction films. Here is a brief listing of a few significant feature films which characterize the political role of the movie industry during and after the so-called the McCarthy era.

THE CONSPIRATOR, 90 min., black and white, 1950.

A terrible film, but very typical of a whole genre of movies that portrayed a deadly Communist conspiracy. Elizabeth Taylor discovers that her military expert husband, Robert Taylor, is a Soviet agent. Other films about villainous "closet" Communists like *My Son John* (1952) and *I Was a Communist for the FBI* (1951) are not available in 16mm.

The Conspirator can be rented from Films Inc.

TRIAL, 107 min., black and white, 1955.

This is one of the few intelligently made, rational, and complex depictions of a Communist threat to American institutions. The film treats the trial of a young Mexican-American who is duped into becoming a martyr for a Communist organization. This is probably the only anti-Communist movie of the decade that can still be viewed without embarrassment.

Rental from Films Inc.

SWEET SMELL OF SUCCESS, 96 min., black and white, 1957.

With the decline of Senator McCarthy in 1954 and the gradual warming of the Cold War, Hollywood began to rebound from its right-wing propaganda of earlier in the decade. This film, written by the once blacklisted Clifford Odets, is a shattering portrayal of a red-baiting, Broadway columnist and his shifty press agent. It

Sweet Smell of Success

United Artists

represents one of the earliest attempts to expose right-wing influence on the entertainment world. The acting in this film is also something to behold, with Burt Lancaster and Tony Curtis as the evil pair. Highly recommended as one of the bravest movies of the decade.

Rental from United Artists 16.

THE INVASION OF THE BODY SNATCHERS, 80 min., black and white, 1956.

This is typical of the genre of alien invasion sci-fi movies that—consciously or unconsciously—symbolized the national fears of Communist subversion in the fifties. For more information, see the chapter on science fiction films.

Rental from Ivy Films or Hurlock Cine World.

There are other approaches a teacher can use to study the fifties besides those recommended here, but the films of the decade itself should be crucial to any survey. In a sense, the social history of movies is the social history of our culture. Keeping this in mind, I wonder how students in 1996 will interpret the connection of "supercop" movies of the seventies to the Watergate syndrome. I somehow just can't imagine a TV show about contemporary times called *Happy Days*. But then, back in 1954, with a shaky peace in Korea, Joe McCarthy, recession, the Sherman Adams scandal, and the school desegregation crisis in Little Rock, who'd have thought that all people would remember was Uncle Miltie and "Rock Around the Clock"?

13
Women on Film

The women's liberation movement is having an impact on the American educational mainstream. In many secondary schools and colleges all over the country, basic social studies and English classes are featuring lessons, units, mini-courses, and, in some cases, entire semesters devoted to an analysis of the role of women in society. Books such as Betty Friedan's *The Feminine Mystique* and Robin Morgan's *Sisterhood Is Powerful* are becoming popular reading requirements, and *Ms.* magazine is being cited as a kind of portable curriculum.

One of the goals of women's studies is to examine ways American women have been traditionally discriminated against (economically, politically, culturally, socially) and to analyze ways in which they can attain a more positive role in society.

A recent popular approach to this phase of women's studies has been an analytical study of the roles of women portrayed in American commercial films. Courses devoted to this are particularly popular on the college level (see references to such courses in the American Film Institute's

Guide to College Courses in Film and Television (Acropolis, 1973, 1975). This type of film study examines how female "types" were created, largely by male writers and directors, and portrayed on the screen. The traditional movie female—from the Jean Harlow-Marilyn Monroe sex goddess to the stock heroine of Westerns, swashbucklers, and gangster films—was always carried off into the sunset by the stalwart, masculine hero. Even the independent pants-wearing Katherine Hepburns and Rosalind Russells generally ended their pictures by sacrificing careers and status for "the right guy."

A study of films for their social and intellectual content can provide a revealing glimpse of attitudes and mores. American films certainly reflect male society's domination (real and wishful) over women, and because of their tremendous popularity, movies have helped propagandize female dependency. In many college courses in women's studies old movies personifying negative female stereotypes are screened. One very popular course of this kind screened *Grand Hotel* (a compilation of stock female soap opera problems), *Mildred Pierce* (career girls can't win), *Pillow Talk* (the Doris Day syndrome), *High Noon* (Grace Kelly's mealy-mouthed heroine), and *The Seven-Year Itch* (Marilyn Monroe as sex object). Teachers wanting to focus their own women-on-film units on this theme of negative stereotypes could have a field day, since examples are endless.

While I agree in principle with this approach, I'm not sure it will be too effective with secondary school students. One reason is that students will have to spend a lot of time viewing bad movies. (*Pillow Talk* and *Mildred Pierce* are cinematically awful!)

Another problem is the students themselves. Junior and senior high school students—particularly the males—are probably not sophisticated or sensitive enough to feminist issues to spot all the stereotypes and negative images. It's one

I'm No Angel

thing to criticize a dated Stepin Fetchit image of a black
man—most of today's kids couldn't miss that stereotype. But
asking adolescents how Doris Day's sacrificing of her career
and individuality to Rock Hudson's manliness is anti-female
is something else! I sense that female stereotype studies work
well with college students because they are already sensitized
to basic feminist issues. Betty Friedan, Kate Millet, and
Gloria Steinem have already affected them.

The role I see for film in secondary school women's
studies is slightly different. The following are a few quality
films that present, in a variety of ways, realistic female
problems and points of view. These films can be used as sen-
sitizers for students who have had little exposure to the
positive aspects of women's liberation. Values-oriented discussion should follow the screening of each film, analyzing
the situation of the female protagonists and how this relates
to the changing role of women in society today. After
students have engaged in this type of film study, they can
begin to attack female stereotypes and negative images.

Recommended Films

If you intend to show all these films, try to arrange them in the order in which they are listed here, since they tend to complement each other.

THE GODDESS, 105 min., black and white, 1958.

This is one of the most underrated films of any genre. Its topic is the ultimate movie sex symbol—the blonde, slinky, Hollywood queen, a composite Harlow-Monroe-Novak. It is, however, a humanistic portrait of the soul of such a woman. Kim Stanley portrays this symbolic screen beauty as a rootless, emotionally insecure victim of her physical attributes.

The film (based on an original script by Paddy Chayefsky) shows her rise from foster child to local bauty contestant to star, yet it constantly focuses on her as a victim. She is the perennial sex object to her lovers, her fans, and to society. The film parallels the real career of Marilyn Monroe, including the prophetic ending. Show this film to illustrate the manipulation of women as commercial objects. (Though *The Goddess* is adult in content, it contains no nudity or profanity).

Rental from Macmillan Audio Brandon Films.

THE HIRED HAND, 90 min., color, 1971.

A wandering cowboy (Peter Fonda, who also directed the film) leaves his trailmate to return to his wife and child he deserted years before. At first his wife rejects him, forcing him to work as a hired hand. Gradually the relationship grows, and she takes him back, only to lose him again as he rides off to aid his ex-comrade in a gunfight. Although *The Hired Hand* is superficially about male comradeship, its most important character is the wife, who is brilliantly portrayed by Verna Bloom and is the personification of the real Western heroine. Her basic need throughout the film is to survive in the harsh frontier environment. Companionship is part of this survival. Her neighbors chastise her for seeking companionship with several men during her husband's long absence. When he returns and they are reunited, the companionship is normalized again. By the time he leaves and dies, the audience has come to understand that this woman is not to be judged. In the last scene of the film, she

sits on her porch expecting news of her husband's death. The friend
he died saving rides into the yard. The camera closes in on her
resolved, almost satisfied expression. It is no accident that the
friend is riding her husband's horse. She will survive. *The Hired
Hand* is an excellent vehicle for discussions on double standards of
behavior which discriminate against women. It is also a realistic,
humane portrayal of frontier women.

Rental from Twyman Films and Universal 16.

RACHEL, RACHEL, 104 min., color, 1968.

Directed by Paul Newman and starring Joanne Woodward,
this well-known film is a moving portrait of the spinster syndrome.
Rachel is an over-30 "old maid" schoolteacher, struggling for a
rewarding existence in a society that seems to have no room for
single women. Although the film is sad (Rachel's attempt at a love
affair flounders, and even when she willingly accepts the fact that
she might have an illegitimate child, the pregnancy turns out to be a
tumor), it never turns into a soap opera. *Rachel, Rachel* raises all
kinds of questions about the alternatives available to an unmarried
woman in our society.

Rental from Twyman Films, Macmillan Audio Brandon
Films, and Swank Motion Pictures.

THE PUMPKIN EATER, 110 min., black and white, 1964.

This is a blistering screen portrait of the female divorcée and
her problems. Anne Bancroft plays a woman who has been married
three times and has eight children. The story is depicted totally
from her point of view, pointing out all the frustrations confronting
women in this position. It raises some fundamental questions about
the status of women in society and the burdens they must bear. It
also emphasizes the important point that marriage is no panacea.

Rental from Macmillan Audio Brandon Films, Twyman
Films, Swank Motion Pictures, and Contemporary Films-
McGraw-Hill.

THE WOMEN, 134 min., black and white, 1939.

This movie version of Clare Boothe Luce's popular comedy is
a combination of a realistic statement by women of their need to be
positive forces in society and a mélange of old-time movie

stereotypes. I've seen audiences react to it both ways, and part of the reason is that it contains both liberated and stereotyped characters. Still, the film can serve as a valuable discussion starter.

Rental from Films Inc.

I'M NO ANGEL, 88 min., black and white, 1933.

Mae West was unique among Hollywood sex symbols. Unlike the fragile heroine of *The Goddess,* Mae West was a happy-go-lucky, strong willed individual who was never dominated by any man, on- or off-screen. She was the "auteur" of her films, writing her own dialogue and selecting her directors and male stars. In this film—one of her funniest—she exerts her will on Cary Grant. I recommend at least one Mae West film in any unit on women's studies because of the unique, dominant image she projected. This was one woman no man was ever going to build a picket fence around.

Rental of *I'm No Angel* (as well as Mae West's other films) from Universal 16.

The Women

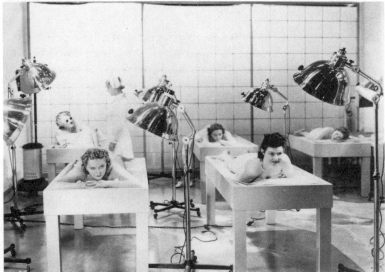

One final note: Another potentially interesting approach to women on film would be to study the works of female directors to see how they handle the stereotypes. The problem, however, is that until recently few females have directed commercial films. Also, two of our best female filmmakers—Shirley Clarke and Elaine May—have generally dealt with male themes and points of view. Still, for those interested in the works of female filmmakers (who, I believe, will eventually be a tremendous force in the movie industry), *Film Comment* magazine's November 1972, issue has published a detailed filmography of the cinematic works of women. Write to: *Film Comment,* Box 686, Village Station, Brookline, Mass. 02147.

14
Sport and Society

With increasing flexibility in high school social studies and, to an even greater extent, English curricula, high interest mini-courses and electives are springing up everywhere. But when I initiated a four-week social studies mini-course called "Sport and Society," back in 1972, I can recall many of my colleague's skeptical reactions—"What have sports got to do with what we teach?" "Where are the implications for civics, history, or economics?" "Looks like another of Maynard's movie specials!"

Having used a number of unconventional methods during my seven-year tenure in the social studies department—almost all of which were related to film—I was not dismayed by my colleagues' cynicism. I saw the analysis of sports as a study of a microcosm of our entire way of life. Such an analysis touches on competition (social and economic), hero worship and mythology, race relations, criminology (most organized gambling centers around sports), international relations (the Olympics syndrome), and women's rights. To me, this was an ideal social studies unit; yet in 1972 (and possibly even now), to a lot of members of my profession "it wasn't social studies enough."

There were other reasons I chose the subject besides its relevance to the curriculum. I was teaching seniors, and it was January, the official beginning of graduation year. Post-Christmas doldrums and general midyear weariness had set in, for me as well as the students. A subject like sports had built-in motivational appeal and seemed like a perfect way to reestablish communication lines between my students and me.

To start the mini-course I gave the class a list of popular books on sports and asked each student to read one. The school librarian helped by ordering additional paperback copies of each title and putting them on reserve for the class. The books they chose from were:*

Jim Bouton. *Ball Four* (Dell).

A best selling "inside story" on baseball by a genuinely funny and intelligent ex-athlete. (I should add that of all the books on the list, Bouton's was the most popular, particularly among the girls.)

Dave Meggyssy. *Out of Their League* (Paperback Library).

An ex-football player's brutal condemnation of his sport. The students liked this book, which was the first of a series of anti-sports, athlete memoirs. Still, I hesitate to recommend it now since it has become very dated. Meggyssy was a late-blooming flower child of the 60s who spent a summer under the tutelage of the now notorious Jack Scott. Meggyssy's protest against the dehumanizing nature of football recruiting and the "piece of meat" philosophy of most team owners toward players is admirable. And, he had the courage of his convictions by quitting his high paying job with the St. Louis Cardinals. But his conversion to radicalism and his acceptance of drug culture are not very well explained. Readers are left with the impression that Meggyssy switched from big dumb jock to big dumb radical. Still, in 1972 the book was truly revolutionary.

---

*Since I taught this unit a number of other useful books and films have become available. A list of additional suggestions appears at the end of this chapter.

Jesse Owens. *Blackthink* (Pocket Books).

A memoir written by the noted black track star and 1936 Olympics hero and a traditional defense of American amateur sports.

Jack Olsen. *The Black Athlete* (Pyramid).

This compilation of articles from *Sports Illustrated* exposes the subtle and not-so-subtle racism in amateur and professional athletics. This book holds up very well today, apparently because much of what Olsen exposed is still prevalent.

Harry Edwards. *The Revolt of the Black Athlete* (Free Press).

A black sociologist's manifesto for a boycott of the Olympics by black athletes. This is a little dated now, and Olsen's book covers the same territory.

Ted Williams. *My Turn at Bat* (Pocket Books).

An outspoken memoir, but typical "I owe it all to the game" stuff.

After reading assignments were made, I presented a series of films that examined various aspects of sports and their impact on society. First we saw a brief film of profootball highlights (this type of film is available from the promotion department of any team office). Student reaction was instant and positive. Player recognition and admiration for physical strength dominated the post-screening discussion. Everyone agreed that football was exciting, though a few students did question the difference between excitement and violence.

I followed this with one of the most beautiful (and controversial) of all sports films, *Olympia, 1936.*

OLYMPIA 1936, Part I, 95 min., Part II, 95 min., 1936-38, Germany.

Commissioned by the Nazi government and directed by Leni Riefensthal, it captures all of the physical grandeur of the 1936 Olympics in Berlin with stunning cinematic effects. The film is both a brilliant tribute to athletic prowess and a heavily propagandistic statement of Nazi racial mythology. (The prejudiced cameras, however, cannot mask the fact that the true heroes of these games were

MOMA

Olympia, 1936

not the Aryan athletes, but the predominately black American track team, led by the incomparable Jesse Owens.) I used only sections of this three-hour film (specifically reel 1 of Part I, which includes a lengthy Nazi-oriented prologue to the games, and the black American track victories; and reel 3 of Part II, containing the famous slow-motion diving sequences that equate athletes to gods). These sections prompted much student discussion on the paradoxical nature of the Olympics and the politics of athletic institutions.

Rental from Contemporary Films-McGraw-Hill.

By this time the analytical goals of the unit had become clear to the class—there was a lot more to sports than simple entertainment.

I then presented three dramatic feature films and a short dealing with various interpretations of the role of the athlete in society.

THE LONELINESS OF THE LONG-DISTANCE RUNNER, 103 min., black and white, 1962.

This is a classroom staple of mine. It's the story of a young delinquent whose rehabilitation at a borstal (reformatory) consists of training to win a cross-country race. The film is a highly unconventional interpretation of the "sports builds men" cliche, since the youth halts before the finish line, well ahead of his opponents, and deliberately refuses to win. The film exposes many of the psychological ramifications of sports, particularly the vicarious experiences of the spectators. It makes the statement that there isn't much difference in the eyes of society between an athlete and a race horse.

Rental from Twyman Films.

THE HARDER THEY FALL, 109 min., black and white, 1956.

The story is based on Budd Schulberg's fictionalized version of the Primo Carnera heavyweight boxing scandals of the early thirties. This film presents a shattering portrait of ring corruption, demonstrating that most fighters are merely "pieces of meat" to crooked promoters, managers, and gamblers. Humphrey Bogart, as a conscience-stricken publicist for a corrupt fight syndicate, makes a moving plea at the end of the film for the abolition of boxing. This is a brutal film, but its factual basis makes it particularly thought-provoking.

Rental from Contemporary Films-McGraw-Hill, Macmillan Audio Brandon Films, or Twyman Films.

DOWNHILL RACER, 102 min., color, 1969.

The final film examined the role of the athlete from a completely different light. Intensely competitive and fiercely individualistic, Robert Redford as a champion skier is also a prototype of many athletes. He truly believes that winning is everything. There is nothing likable about this character, except his ability to ski. Although his coach (Gene Hackman) preaches team effort and sportsmanship, in the end he too demonstrates that nothing really matters but victory. This film is not a strong indictment of sports, but it raises many questions concerning the standard cliches about heroic athletes.

Rental from Films Inc.

JEFFRIES-JOHNSON 1910, 21 min., black and white, 1971.

This short documentary covers the early championship of the legendary black boxer Jack Johnson and the efforts of formerly retired champ Jim Jeffries to defeat him in the name of "white racial athletic superiority." Jeffries lost. This film, comprising still photos and some rare movie footage, is an excellent commentary on racism in sports and is preferable to the cumbersome film version of *The Great White Hope.*

Purchase or rental from Contemporary Films-McGraw-Hill.

All the films and books prompted exciting class discussions. During the month of January more materials were added to the already overloaded curriculum: the Super Bowl (and the racial overtones of the Duane Thomas incident), the Winter Olympics' skiers' scandal, involving amateurs endorsing ski equipment, a championship fight, and the NBA All-Star Game. (Similar events take place each year and are covered extensively by TV and in newspapers.) The class had begun to realize how closely sporting events parallel our national life.

I closed the unit by assigning an essay based on the films and readings, asking students to analyze the negative aspects of sports institutions and to suggest possible reforms.

Additional Material

There are always timely articles in newspapers and magazines on the impact of sports on our society. When I taught this unit, I found articles in *Psychology Today*, the *New York Times,* and other general sources very helpful. Some notable recent material on this subject includes:

Roger Kahn. *The Boys of Summer* (Bantam).

A beautifully written nostalgic portrait of the Brooklyn Dodgers of the 1950s.

William Harrison. *Rollerball Murder* (Signet).

A short story about a brutal sport of the future. The story is much better than the motion picture on which it is based. Available in a collection of Harrison's stories.

Scholastic Contact Sports Unit.

A superb anthology on many of the elements of sports covered in this chapter. Though written at a fifth to sixth grade level, this material would be applicable for students in any secondary school grade.

Here are some feature films that will work well in a sports-society unit.

BODY AND SOUL, 112 min., black and white, 1947.

Possibly the best of all prizefight dramas, this film about an unscrupulous boxer and the lives he wrecks is still a powerful study of the athlete as villain. Starring John Garfield and directed by Robert Rossen (whose *The Hustler*, about the world of poolroom gambling, would also fit in this unit).

Rental from Budget Films. (*The Hustler* is available from Films Inc.)

ROCKY, 124 min., color, 1976.

The antidote to *The Harder They Fall* and *Body and Soul*. This extremely popular movie about a Philadelphia club fighter's Cinderella shot at the heavyweight title is one of the very few films that portray boxing in a favorable light. Here we see the sport as a spiritual uplifter, an opportunity for moral redemption. This may be nonsense, but there's no denying the film's power with audiences.

Rental from United Artists 16.

THE BAD NEWS BEARS, 103 min., color, 1976.

Director Michael Ritchie (*Downhill Racer, The Candidate*) has taken a middling script about a bunch of foul-mouthed, preadolescent misfits in Little League baseball and fashioned it into an entertaining and fairly meaningful commentary on American values. Ritchie has structured this tale of winning, losing, and sportsmanship almost totally around the action on the baseball field itself. His ability to tell the story on its own terms, maximizing the sports action, makes the film believable, transcending the fact that virtually all the kids are stage brats who have been seen count-

less times in other films and TV situation comedies. Solid performances by Walter Matthau, as the team's tipsy ex-ballplayer coach,
and Vic Morrow, in the thankless role of a win-crazy parent, help a
great deal.

Rental from Films Inc.

BANG THE DRUM SLOWLY, 105 min., color. 1974.

A fine, touching film about a dying baseball player and the
reaction of his teammates. This potentially maudlin theme is
treated gently, with much emphasis on human comedy. Starring
Robert DiNiro, Michael Moriarity, and Vincent Gardenia.

Rental from Films Inc.

BRIAN'S SONG, 85 min., color, 1973.

The famous TV movie about the relationship between black
and white pro football teammates. Brian Piccolo, the white player
ultimately dies of cancer. Although based on a true story and very
well acted by James Caan and Billy Dee Williams, the film is a bit
on the mawkish side, unlike *Bang the Drum Slowly*. It is a sort of
Love Story with football players.

Rental or lease from Learning Corporation of America.

REQUIEM FOR A HEAVYWEIGHT, 85 min., black and white, 1962.

Rod Serling's classic screenplay about the decline and near fall
of a slow-witted boxer. Although this film is heavily used by
teachers, it might work especially well in a unit on sports.

Rental from Twyman Films, Macmillan Audio Brandon
Films, or Swank Films.

STICKY MY FINGERS, FLEET MY FEET. (see p. 30 for content and
rental information)

15

A Galaxy of Science Fiction Films

In my full-time job as Scholastic's Editorial Director for Language Arts and Humanities I have traveled around the country observing the melange of teaching approaches to secondary school English. Mini-courses and elective programs are a definite trend in English curriculum, though there is an enormous variation from school to school in the kinds of course offerings available. But there is one mini-course elective that most schools seemed to be consistently offering—science fiction. I once attended a workshop on teaching a sci fi elective at the New York State Council of English Teachers convention. The room where the workshop was held had a seating capacity for about 60 people. I'm not exaggerating when I say that at least three times that number of teachers jammed into the room and crowded around the doorway to hear a panel discuss schemes for developing science fiction electives in junior and senior high.

Student interest in such courses is high, and English teachers are recognizing this. More and more, educational publishers are distributing materials for the science fiction literature market. Bantam Books, for instance, publishes a handy guide to teaching this genre, and there are now numerous science fiction anthologies available for schools.

In keeping with this interest, I have developed for this chapter recommendations for what I consider the best science fiction feature films available for classroom use. I have divided my filmography into genres—alien invasion, futuristic, outer space exploration, and ecological—for the sake of convenience. I have not dealt with "mad scientist" epics since these may more adequately fit the horror genre, which, incidentally, is also becoming a popular English mini-course.

Alien Invasion

These films deal with "beings" from other planets attempting to sabotage and infiltrate earth. Movies of this type were particularly popular during the early and mid-fifties and can be analyzed as reflections of McCarthyist fears of "Communist" conspiracies in the United States. Few films of this type are made now.

THE INVASION OF THE BODY SNATCHERS, 80 min., black and white, 1956.

The quintessential alien invasion movie, scary as all get out and full of McCarthyist paranoia. Mysterious seed pods land on earth and produce duplicate humans who intend to sabotage the planet. One minute the next door neighbor is himself, the next minute he only looks like himself but is really a monstrous invader. Tomorrow it could be your wife, you brother, who knows? No study of the genre can be complete without this classic.

Rental from Ivy Films.

THE THING (FROM ANOTHER WORLD), 88 min., black and white, 1951.

The earth is invaded by a ferocious monster capable of limitless reproduction. To compound the problem, this "thing" is made of vegetable matter and can't be killed. Plus, it thrives on human blood. A courageous team of Air Force men confront the monster at a polar research station. This movie is something of a Hollywood legend and became the model for others of its genre in the fifties. *Mad* magazine once did a great spoof of it, portraying a giant carrot on the loose.

Rental from Films Inc.

WAR OF THE WORLDS, 85 min., color, 1953.

A well-made, up-dated version of H.G. Wells' frightening novel of invaders from Mars (*not* based on the famous Orson Welles radio program). This film also has some interesting 1950ish attitudes toward the atomic bomb.

Rental from Films Inc.

THE DAY THE EARTH STOOD STILL, 92 min., black and white, 1951.

Here's a switch—the interplanetary invader (played by the urbane Michael Rennie) is a good guy who comes to earth (Washington, D.C.) to show earthlings how to limit their armaments and work toward peace. A literate, intelligently made film, which is kind of a counteroffensive to the right-wing elements of this genre.

Rental from Films Inc.

Futuristic

This category on sci fi films portrays futuristic visions of life on earth. These films are particularly interesting when examined from the perspective of the times in which they were filmed—for instance, a view of the future from Germany in the 1920s or from England in the thirties. Also worthy of study is the fact that most of these visions of the future are extremely negative. I should note that two of the most famous futuristic novels— *1984* and *Fahrenheit 451*—have been made into second-rate films; and Aldous Huxley's classic *Brave New World* has never been filmed.

METROPOLIS, 120 min., black and white (silent), 1926.

Fritz Lang's famous silent German film of a horrifying,

Things to Come

machine-dominated totalitarian society is still fascinating. It is particularly interesting to consider this film in the context of its time and place. Is it a reflection of rising facism or an ominous warning against it?

Rental from Macmillan Audio Brandon Films, Films Inc.

THINGS TO COME, 92 min., black and white, 1936.

H.G. Wells adapted his own novel in this screenplay, which portrays Great Britain in the future. The film chronicles an atomic war from a mid-thirties point of view, and it is full of meaningful predictions about the world of the seventies. *Things to Come* was directed by William Cameron Menzies, who was later to be art director for *Gone with the Wind* and *The Wizard of Oz*. Naturally the sets and gadgetry of *Things to Come* are spectacular.

Rental from Budget Films and Images, Inc.

THE TRANSATLANTIC TUNNEL, 94 min., black and white, 1935.

A British B movie of the thirties, full of dazzling special effects. The film deals with a team of scientists' efforts to build a sub-ocean tunnel from London to New York. It is also interesting because it has an optimistic message as the tunnel is completed, linking the continents.

Rental from Janus Films.

BETWEEN TIME AND TIMBUKTU, 90 min., color, 1971.

Kurt Vonnegut scripted this made-for-TV film, which utilizes elements of several of his popular works (including *Cat's Cradle* and *Slaughterhouse 5*). While somewhat uneven in quality, it does provide a humorous element to this basically grim genre and would work well in any sci fi unit.

Rental from New Line Cinema.

Outer Space

No sci fi unit could be complete without something from this category, though with the exception of *2001*, films of this type are generally of low quality and are mere extensions of the monstrous alien theme.

THE FLASH GORDON SERIALS, 3 different serials, each containing 12 to 15 chapters, about 15 minutes per chapter, 1938-1940 and

THE BUCK ROGERS SERIAL, 12 chapters, about 15 minutes per chapter, 1936.

These two serials are based on the most popular science fiction comic strips of the thirties and forties. Full of hokey gimmicks and ham acting, serials like these portray life on other planets as a combination of technological utopia and medieval feudalism. I don't recommend a teacher showing an entire serial, but an individual chapter or two might be worthwhile.

These serials are also available in an abbreviated feature film format at about 90 minutes each.

Rental from Ivy Films.

DESTINATION MOON, 91 min., color, 1950.

An interesting, unusually prophetic depiction of interplanetary travel, loaded with accurate details. This inexpensively made, low-key film was a great sleeper in the early fifties and still looks quite good today.

Rental from Ivy Films.

PLANET OF THE APES, 112 min., color, 1967.

This extremely popular film needs no summary. Suffice to say if not taken too seriously it makes some interesting points about evolution and contains some fine elements of satirical humor.

Rental from Films Inc. This film spawned four, generally inferior, sequels that are also available from Films Inc.

2001: A SPACE ODYSSEY, 160 min., color, 1968.

The greatest of all science fiction films (indeed one of the greatest of all films), Stanley Kubrick's astounding vision of the next phase of evolution should almost be required in this kind of course. However, the film is very expensive to rent, and it really loses a great deal visually through the limitations of 16mm. Still if a class can afford it. . .

Rental from Films Inc.

STAR WARS, 120 min., color, 1977.

A big screen, very loud, mammoth budget version of Flash Gordon. This film has an undeniable charm and was very popular at the box office, though in a unit of this kind its primary value would be as an example of the influence of nostalgia on science fiction.

Rental (very expensive) from Films Inc.

Ecological Sci Fi

This last category contains films that ominously warn that human's abuse of the environment may someday haunt them. The best films of this type were made in the fifties, and they all reflect fears resulting from the testing of the bomb.

Incredible Shrinking Man

Universal

More recently Hollywood has tried to portray timelier ecological problems such as overpopulation—*Z.P.G.* and *Soylent Green*—and air pollution—*No Blade of Grass*. These films, however, are so badly done that they cannot be recommended.

THEM! 75 min., black and white, 1954.

One of the earliest examples of this category, *Them!* horrifyingly portrays the effects of radiation on the atmosphere. As a result of atomic testing, red ants grow to monstrous size and march across the country destroying everything in sight. A harrowing, sensationalistic film, as are others of its type.

Rental from Twyman Films or Macmillan Audio Brandon Films.

THE INCREDIBLE SHRINKING MAN, 81 min., black and white, 1957.

This is one of the most underrated, little known pieces of fine cinema of the past twenty-five years. Teachers seeking good science fiction material should be particularly interested in this adaptation of Richard Matheson's novel about a man who mysteriously begins to shrink after exposure to radiation. The hero's survival includes his efforts to thwart a ferocious house cat and a spider. The ending of the film is extremely powerful as the hero ultimately fades into oblivion. This is not just a cheap Hollywood pot boiler. It makes some strong statements about ecology and survival and should generate a great deal of creative writing and discussion among students.

Rental from Universal 16.

THE BIRDS, 119 min., color, 1963.

Alfred Hitchcock's version of the Daphne du Maurier short story about the sudden, violent hostility of birds toward human beings. The film, like the story, offers no explanation for the birds' rampage and is probably closer to pure horror than science fiction. Still teachers dealing with this ecology category may find it useful, and it leaves lots of room for interpretive discussion. (See chapter 10 on teaching literature with film for another approach.)

Rental from Universal 16, Twyman Films, or Swank Films.

16

An Old Man, an Eskimo, and the Rolling Stones: A Unit on Social Ethics

A study of social ethics is often a part of an English or sociology curriculum. Discussion of concepts of right and wrong, doing one's duty, and the like generally give students a chance to express personal feelings and attitudes. Many great works of literature—*Hamlet, Antigone,* and *The Ox-Bow Incident* to name just a few—can stimulate this kind of discussion. So can films (and they may be even more effective with reluctant readers) or a combination of films and literature.

Once I was required each year to teach a unit on ethical problems, and the one I'm about to describe involved three feature films of totally different subject matter. I began the unit for average senior high social studies students with a few lessons on cultural anthropology, demonstraing that ethics are based largely on a culture's adaptation to its physical environment. Hence ideas of right and wrong may be relative to conditions within a particular culture. A classic example of this is a study of the Eskimo tradition of wife-sharing as a form of hospitality. In Western culture such a custom would be condemned as adultery. Why does it exist among Eskimos? What happens when it conflicts with Western culture? How can we understand such a foreign custom without condemning it?

There is a marvelous, little known feature film dealing with these questions called *The Savage Innocents* (color, 90 min., 1961; rental from Films Inc.). Starring Anthony Quinn as an Eskimo hunter, this simply made film explains the nature of the Eskimo culture by tracing the harsh life-style of its members. The film examines the relationship between men and women in a culture where women are in the minority as a result of the practice of first-born female infanticide, which the film explains. The long Arctic night and the unending quest for food in a frozen wasteland leave little time for diversion. The lonely hunter, away from his home, who is, after all, one of the men (as the Eskimos call themselves), is treated by his "brothers" to their dearest possessions. The lending of one's wife to "laugh" with a visitor is a highly cherished form

The Savage Innocents

MOMA

of hospitality, and the film (through both the convincing actors and a narrator) spells this out. The bulk of the film deals with cross-cultural conflict. A Catholic missionary visits a young Eskimo and his wife. When the missionary refuses to eat his hosts' food (a bowl of maggots) and then condemns the Eskimo for offering his wife, the Eskimo assaults the priest. In the struggle the missionary is accidentally killed. The Eskimo claims, though his intent was not to kill, that the man was "rude." Western society, symbolized by the policeman who hunts the Eskimo down, does not see that as a valid excuse. The rest of the film provides the viewer with an interesting portrait of conflicting ethics.

The Savage Innocents works with students on a variety of levels. Its narrative is clear and simple, yet its anthropological information is quite accurate. (It is based on the highly regarded anthropological novel *Top of the World* by Hans Ruesch.) In addition to teaching about the customs of an alien culture, it raises excellent discussion questions about our own culture and how it relates to others.

I showed the film in three parts (a reel a day, as I did with the other films in this unit), assigning a couple of brief questions after each section. Though this method destroys the cinematic flow—a problem teachers must learn to cope with since too few schools have flexible enough scheduling patterns to show a 100-minute feature—it provides day-to-day continuity. Also, stringing films out in this manner helps keep attendance regular and motivates potential truants to at least come back three days in a row.

After some very intense class discussion and debate on the Eskimo's guilt or innocence and an open-ended essay assignment on the film, I altered the unit a bit. I showed two additional feature films that raised ethical questions about the nature of American culture.

The film version of Robert Anderson's play, *I Never Sang for My Father* (color, 97 min., 1971; rental from

Twyman

I Never Sang for My Father

Twyman Films, Macmillan Audio Brandon Films and Swank Films), should be well known to many teachers. The October 1971 issue of Scholastic's *Literary Cavalcade* reprinted the play, and I know of many classrooms where it is taught. I showed the film version to motivate student examination of the problems of generation gap and our society's treatment of the aged. It's a story of a forty-year-old son's (Gene Hackman) difficulties in trying to live his own life while coping with an often tyrannical, eighty-year-old father (Melvin Douglas), and it raises deep ethical questions that students too often never think about. What should society do for its aged population? Is it morally committed to provide a viable life for old people beyond keeping them medically alive? Are children ethically required to care for aged parents? What alternatives exist to our present system of caring for the aged?

Are institutions for the aged possible solutions? Why? Why not?

After seeing the film, the class discussed these questions and individual members role-played the father-and-son relationship in an effort to "feel" the situation involved. One follow-up activity we used was to have a group of students portray sons and daughters trying to tell their aged parents they were to be sent to an old folks home, while other students, as the parents, reacted.

Another discussion activity the class engaged in related back to *The Savage Innocents*. In that film the treatment of the aged in Eskimo culture was shown when Inuk's (Anthony Quinn) aging mother-in-law indicated that her hands were becoming paralyzed. Without emotion she asked him to leave her on the ice so that the polar bear could find her. As nourishment for the bear, she, in turn, would provide nourishment for her family, which would hunt the bear for its meat and fur. This fatalistic approach was crucial to the survival of the Eskimo and hence becomes understandable when analyzed by outsiders. Most of the students indicated that such a solution to old age problems would *not* work in our culture, though they were perplexed after seeing *I Never Sang for My Father*. Certainly we do not have a satisfactory system for our senior citizens.

In conclusion I assigned an essay asking students to imagine themselves past sixty-five and to state how they wanted to spend the remainder of their lives.

I must add that a film such as *I Never Sang for My Father* has other excellent classroom uses. A cross-media study involving Anderson's play and the way the film heightens the story dramatically would be an interesting approach. (There is a scene in the film only in which the son visits institutions for the aged that is positively frightening). This film has a humanizing effect on kids about a subject with which they are generally not concerned.

To conclude my cinematic treatment of social ethics, I showed a controversial film about the so-called youth culture. *Gimme Shelter* (color, 90 min., 1970, Cinema V, PG; apply for special high school rate) is allegedly a documentary film about the Rolling Stones' United States tour in the fall of 1969. However, its real subject matter is the young audience the British rock group attracts. The focal point of *Gimme Shelter* is the infamous incident at Altamont Speedway, near San Francisco, where the Stones and their managers staged a "free concert" attracting nearly 300,000 youths from across the country. Refusing police aid, those responsible for the event hired a group of Hell's Angels to keep order. The result was half rock show, half violent freak out with hundreds of people beaten and one man killed, stabbed by a Hell's Angel who claimed the man was approaching the stage with a gun.

Since two-thirds of *Gimme Shelter* concentrates directly on the nonconformist behavior of the young crowds (everything from long hair to public taking of drugs), it provides a vivid portrait of American youth counterculture. Thus, students can examine some of the reasons for the alienation of such a large segment of the population. I should add that there are brief scenes of nudity and violence that might be offensive to some students, and the class should be cautioned ahead of time.

Far more relevant in a unit on ethical problems, however, is to analyze the ethics of the makers of *Gimme Shelter*. Although the filmmakers may not have planned it that way, this is a very tragic movie, and its narrative structure helps emphasize the tragedy. It begins with the Rolling Stones watching themselves on a film viewer, reliving the events of the tour. At the very start the audience is told of the violence of Altamont and the killing, and the film then flashes back to the events step by step. The cameras dwell on the most grotesque characters in the massive crowd, and the editing definitely heightens the drama of all the violence. The

Gimme Shelter

New York Times film critic, Vincent Canby, accused the makers of *Gimme Shelter,* David and Albert Maysles, of exploiting the events and helping to create them. His review of the film, "Making Murder Pay" (*New York Times,* January 13, 1970, sect. 2, p. 3), raised many questions about the ethics of documentary filmmakers, and we used it as an additional source for discussion.

17

The Not-So-Hidden Persuaders: TV Commercials in the Curriculum

As an instructor in film media education and lecturer to various teacher groups around the country, I'm continually badgered by a constant complaint from my audience: "We have no money for any film or media resources in our school." Although I have dealt with the problems of funding earlier in this book, I'd like to point out again that even the most hard pressed teachers have one great media source at their disposal without cost—the television commercial.

The TV commercial is a genuine microcosm of all media study. It is a highly developed, sophisticated 35mm film (in most cases) that incorporates all the professional polish of any major Hollywood film. (Stanley Kubrick once said that if he could command half the production budget, per minute, of the average TV commercial, he could produce a feature film more technically stunning than anything he's ever done. And Kubrick made *2001: A Space Odyssey*.) Commercials, in addition, represent a very effective form of scripting. Imagine being able to tell a complete story—with a beginning, middle, and an end, which usually features the resolution of a conflict, in 60 seconds!

The TV commercial is also a key to understanding the politics and economics of the television medium. Programming is based on pre-sold time spots, and network policies, TV ratings, and commercials are all intricately tied together. (In 1975 the popular show *Gunsmoke* was canceled by CBS after a 20-year run. Curiously, *Gunsmoke's* rating had not slipped out of the top 10. The reason for its cancellation was based on the show's primary appeal to rural and older audiences—groups who do not represent top consumers throughout the country. Hence, major advertisers whose commercials concentrate on appeals to younger and more urban populations were no longer interested in sponsoring *Gunsmoke.*) For students to understand the nature of TV programming, a knowledge of the advertising influences in that medium is essential.

The impact of the television commercial extends even beyond its cinematic and video elements. It saturates the airwaves. It conditions buying habits. It "teaches." It entertains. It annoys. It reflects the American character. It distorts it. The television commercial is, in short, a national institution.

Because of this impact of commercials on mass media—and because they represent the cheapest audio-visual source teachers can find (just turn on a TV set)—they make excellent classroom tools for a number of curriculum purposes. Here are a few examples from my own classroom experience:

Consumer Economics

Obviously the first and foremost purpose of 30, 60, or 90 seconds of TV advertising is to create a demand for the product on display. For a study of consumerism, a teacher might begin with Vance Packard's old, but still timely book *The Hidden Persuaders* (Pocket Books, 1957). All its examples are dated (it was written almost two decades ago), but the book's analysis of the emotional nature of consumer buying habits is still essentially accurate. Packard chronicled the advertising industry's pioneering research in the 1950s on consumer image appeal, and he described, in detail, the early psychological experiments in motivational research. The best parts of the book deal with the increasing standardization of most products and how people identify what they buy with the subconscious images the product projects to them. The chapter on giving products "personalities" is still very provocative.

Teachers could use a classroom set of *The Hidden Persuaders,* eliminating some of the more dated chapters and those including the author's moralizing (a consistent flaw in all of Packard's books), or they could adapt the content to a few colorful classroom presentations, using some contemporary commercials as examples of the timeliness of the "persuaders' principle." To impress on students how closely people identify products with images and how great an impact commercials have on viewers, teachers can use what I call a "slogan skim." This consists of listing a number of standard commercial sales pitches and asking students to cite the products they represent. Here are a few standards of the past. (Since these watchwords change frequently, teachers should try to keep running lists of popular current slogans):

"Aren't you glad you use —————? Don't you wish everybody did?"

"You've got a lot to live and ————— got a lot to give."

"The Un-Cola —————."

"The Wings of Man —————."

"The Beetle —————."

"Try it, you'll like it —————."

Invariably the names of the products will be household words to students. Some kids know entire commercials by heart (if only they had such memories of literature or rules of grammar!). Once it has been established how much a part of the national personality these advertisements are, students can begin to analyze their effects on consumer buying habits.

Sociology
With this framework students can examine how commercials reflect American life as it is and how they distort it. The impact of TV advertising beyond its positive economic power was summed up in the famous *Report of the National Advisory Commission on Civil Disorders,* resulting from a study of the urban riots in 1968. The report commented on cultural factors that pressured low-income black households into seeking expensive consumer goods as status symbols, thus leading to overextension of credit in enslaving installment buying. The most significant of these cultural factors, the report concluded, was the saturation of conspicuous consumption through TV advertising, which reinforced have-not attitudes among the poor. The implications were, of course, that commercials reflecting affluent middle-class white American life-styles helped compound the frustrations of the poor. Students should therefore examine individual commercials in depth, noting their potential beyond simple product sales.

Here is a standard group of questions I use in such a study: What product is being sold? What *use* has the product to society? (What does it actually *do?*) What *else* is being marketed besides the product (associated images like sex, youth, status, nostalgia, stereotypes, security, and so forth)? What types of audiences are the sales pitch geared to (age, race, ethnic group, area of the country, social class)? How does the commercial portray American life? What does it say about us as a people? Naturally, teachers can and should combine the sociological study with the economic analysis.

Film-Media Study

As I said earlier, commercials represent the most sophisticated use of the film medium. Hence, they can be integrated into any course on cinema and analyzed for their editing, direction, cinematography, sound, acting, and other elements. In addition, they are ideal models for studies in humor and satire, particularly the numerous spoofs of old movies. After all, some recognition must be given to the astounding fact that TV commercials can project entire dramatic and cinematic entities into 60 seconds or less. No course in film can afford to neglect them.

It might also be pointed out to students that a number of prominent movie and television directors began their careers as makers of commercials. Indeed, some of these individuals still shoot commercials to obtain funds for more important cinematic projects. This is especially true in Europe where such director superstars as Richard Lester *(Hard Day's Night, Petulia, Three Musketeers)* and Gilo Pontecorvo *(The Battle of Algiers)* regularly make commercials. Young and gifted American directors like Howard Zieff *(Slither, Hearts of the West)* and Dick Richards *(Farewell, My Lovely)* began their careers in commercials, and the style and pacing of their feature films reflect this (for better or for worse).

Creative Writing

While this type of activity should be a specific part of any media study course, teachers should also consider using the creative writing aspects of TV commercials in any English class. The process of scripting—both through creation of dialogue and the planning of scenes—has been heralded by several language arts experts as a most lifelike creative writing situation. The sparse style of a commercial script, with its numbered scenes and balance between dialogue (or monologue) and visual action, makes for an ideal writing assignment. Students can work on scripts individually or in groups, simulating an ad agency approach.

One of the best lessons I ever taught revolved around writing a script by applying the principle of "candidate sell." My class of seniors had just read *The Hidden Persuaders* and Joe McGinniss's funny, informative book *The Selling of the President 1968,* on the media campaign, particularly the TV commercials, of Richard Nixon. The latter book is full of actual commercial script examples, and the class was divided into "agency" groups and asked to pick a candidate for president and create a commercial script full of memorable images. The idea of "packaging" candidates is now as common as any form of advertising, and the McGinniss book is a virtual text on the subject. In performing this activity students not only learned the scripting process, but also how to use the techniques of the "persuaders." I highly recommend this approach to writing.

Recommended Sources

Books

Packard, Vance. *The Hidden Persuaders* (Pocket Books, 1957).

McGinniss, Joe. *The Selling of the President 1968* (Pocket Books, 1970).

Della Femina, Jerry. *From Those Wonderful Folks Who Brought You Pearl Harbor* (Avon Books, 1970).
    A very funny, beautifully written memoir of an ad man—his value conflicts, bouts of conscience, and ultimate sense of ethics. A nice antidote to the somber Packard view and much more contemporary.

Mass Communications Arts: Messages and Meaning (Scholastic Book Services).

The second volume of Scholastic's high school media program, which I edited, contains relevant excerpts from Packard, McGinniss, and Della Femina as well as an extensive advertising writing activity.

Films

Clio Awards. The Oscars of TV commercials are called Clios, and they're presented each year to commercials in dozens of categories. The advertising industry makes various reels of award winners available for classrooms at very low rates and even has supporting teaching guides. Teachers with any kind of a film rental budget will find this an outstanding source. For further information contact the American Television and Radio Commercials Festival ("Clio"), 30 East 60th St., New York, N.Y. 10022.

Classic Commercials from the Museum of Modern Art Film Library. Sample reels of old commercials from the 50s and early 60s. Museum of Modern Art.

Sixty Second Spot, 25 min., color, 1974. The making of a 7 Up commercial. For details, see description in short films chapter, page 30.

Television

The classroom set need only to be turned on to find many examples to study.

Sesame Street. This popular and successful program for preschoolers makes extensive use of the principles of TV commercials to "sell" verbal and mathematical concepts. Junior and senior high students of commercials should take a look to see how this process can be applied to education.

❧ 18 ❧
John Ford
and the
American Image

"When the legend becomes a fact," chortled the old newspaper editor in John Ford's film *The Man Who Shot Liberty Valance*, "print the legend." *The Man Who Shot Liberty Valance* is a western, directed by a man whose personality is stamped on a series of the most important and artistic western films ever produced. John Ford's westerns, indeed all of his films, are about legends, heroes, and traditional American values. Most of his films, even the starkly realistic screen version of *The Grapes of Wrath*, have an optimistic, almost romantic belief that the "American dream" will persevere and endure. In some of his later films, however, i.e., *The Man Who Shot Liberty Valance*, the heroes and legends are present, but they are older, more introspective, more complex and even a little jaded.

The career of John Ford, which ended with his death at age 78 in August 1973, spans five decades of film history. To date, no filmmaker in any country has been credited with a finer body of work. Consider his record: classic silents such as *The Iron Horse* and *Three Bad Men;* monumental films of the

'30s including *The Lost Patrol, The Informer, The Hurricane, Young Mr. Lincoln, Stagecoach, The Grapes of Wrath;* of the '40s, *The Long Voyage Home, How Green Was My Valley, Tobacco Road, They Were Expendable, My Darling Clementine, Fort Apache, She Wore a Yellow Ribbon;* of the '50s, *Rio Grande, Wagonmaster, Three Godfathers, The Quiet Man, The Long Gray Line, Mr. Roberts, The Searchers, The Last Hurrah;* and of the '60s, *Two Rode Together, The Man Who Shot Liberty Valance* and *Cheyenne Autumn.* And this is only a partial listing!

If Ford were a novelist, his work would probably be mandatory reading in American literature courses along with Henry James, Faulkner, Steinbeck, and Hemingway. But Ford was *not* an author, he was a movie director. Interestingly, in many English or communications classes where film directors are studied, the names of Bergman, Fellini, Welles, and Kubrick are usually listed more prominently than Ford's. When I raise the subject of John Ford's work with teachers who use film in the classroom, I receive responses such as:

"Oh, most of his films are too old and corny."

They're full of negative stereotypes of Indians and blacks."

"Ford is a right-wing reactionary, and his films show it." (This teacher then made an exception of *The Grapes of Wrath.*)

"Kids don't care about Westerns and Irish nostalgia today."

In their own way these statements about Ford's films are true. In spite of the high regard and awards his films received in their time, they are somewhat dated by today's standards, particularly their highly patriotic values and patronizing stereotypes. Yet, students should examine several examples of John Ford's work for two important reasons.

Personal Cinematic Traits

Ford might be called a "personality" director, that is, certain elements of style recognizable as his personal stamp are present in all of his films. He is also one of the few American directors (Alfred Hitchcock is another) who made films without much Hollywood studio interference. Consequently, Ford was the "author" of his works. He shaped the final celluloid product, blending script, cinematography, acting, music, and editing into what was recognizably his.

There is an old saying that you can look at a film for five minutes and recognize whether it's one of John Ford's. This is largely true. Take his use of actors, for example. The actors in his films comprise a kind of stock company. While watching samples of his work of the past 30 years, these actors turn up again and again in variations of roles to which they had been molded by the director. Harry Carey, Victor McLaglen, Thomas Mitchell, John Wayne (Ford created him!), Henry Fonda, John Carradine, and in later years, Ken Curtis, Ben Johnson, and Woody Strode were all mainstays of Ford's films.

Fonda and Wayne represent two classic screen heroes in John Ford films. Fonda's Abe Lincoln, (*Young Mr. Lincoln*, 1939), Tom Joad (*The Grapes of Wrath*, 1940), Wyatt Earp (*My Darling Clementine*, 1946), and even *Mr. Roberts*, (1955) are all versions of the same character—the shy, modest, logical, quiet American folk hero.

Wayne's screen personality was also molded in John Ford films, particularly as the aging frontiersman in *She Wore a Yellow Ribbon, Rio Grande, The Searchers,* and *The Man Who Shot Liberty Valance*.

Other traits are consistently recognizable in all John Ford films: his use of scenic locations (Utah's Monument Valley in almost all of the westerns); music (themes in his '30s films reappear in later works, creating a series of cross-refer-

Stagecoach

ences from film to film); bawdy Irish humor; single-minded patriotism, which dates much of his work; and portraits of simple people—farmers, pioneers, saddle tramps, cavalry men, sailors, and laborers.

Just as book readers can recognize certain stylistic devices in the body of work of a great novelist, so can "readers" of film recognize these devices in the work of a great director. Unfortunately, some film cultists have elevated this "auteur" stature to far too many undeserving directors.

Reflections of American Society

The other reason students should view samples of Ford's work relates to what these films say about our society. Ford's films are a tapestry of American attitudes and values. They represent our country at its best and its worst. When we look at some of his early and mid '30s films, we perceive some of the basic national attitudes of the past. *Judge Priest* (1936) starred Will Rogers as a rural Kentucky judge who defends a Confederate veteran who had been framed on a murder charge. The film is full of liberal rhetoric about the rights of the defendant, fair play, and defense of the underdog. Rogers, of course, personified these values in real life, and, in this film plus two other Ford pieces *Dr. Bull,* 1933, and *Steamboat Round the Bend,* 1935, became one of the movies' first civil libertarians.

However, there is another side to *Judge Priest* and films like it. For humor, Ford employed the famous black actor Stephin Fetchit, who made a career of playing lowly, comical, superstitious "darkies." To accuse Ford of racism for using a character like this would be unfair since this style of humor and portrayal of blacks was quite common in the '30s and '40s. But such portrayals by today's standards are extremely, and rightly, offensive. As they view a film like *Judge Priest* today, students can see the contradictions in American populism and liberalism of the past, which advocated a democratic society for whites only.

Other, more important Ford films provide similar mirrors of the attitudes of their times. *The Grapes of Wrath* (1940) was based on Steinbeck's searing novel, but Nunnally Johnson's script and Ford's direction altered the work considerably. Although the plight of the Okies is portrayed with graphic realism, the film takes on a hopeful spirit toward the end. By 1940, the New Deal had succeeded in bouying optimism, and the government's Department of Agriculture work camp is portrayed in the film as a ray of hope. The end of the film where Ma Joad asserts that her spirit remains unbroken ("Pa, we're the people.") is a vision of a society that has a determination to survive.

John Ford's westerns also contain interesting portraits of American values. In his early westerns, particularly *Stagecoach* (1939), Ford draws a clear line between good guys and bad guys. But in later films his western heroes begin to change. John Wayne's retiring cavalry captain in *She Wore a Yellow Ribbon* (1948) is the traditional hero grown old and tired. In *The Searchers* (1956), Wayne plays Ethan Edwards, also an aging Frontiersman but a man consumed with vengeance. The Indians who kidnapped Edwards' niece are the

Warner Brothers

The Searchers

bad guys, but the film focuses more on the white man's blind hatred. Ford portrays his hero as a cantankerous, vindictive loner (the film includes lots of shots of Wayne isolated, riding alone) and never tries to milk our sympathy for him.

In *The Man Who Shot Liberty Valance* (1963), Wayne also plays an aging Westerner whose way of life gradually passes him by while his Eastern friend (James Stewart) becomes a politician and the West becomes "civilized." In *Cheyenne Autumn* (1964), Ford's last western, the Indians, who had been stock bad guys in his previous films, become heroes, embodied with many of the traditional Henry Fonda-John Wayne traits. There is a marvelous high angle shot of the mounted Cheyennes riding in line formation across the famous Monument Rock. Ford used this exact shot in several of his previous films, except in them it was the cavalry that crossed the Rock.

By examining Ford's westerns, students can see the changing patterns in American heroism, which reflect the changing values in American life. The films of John Ford belong in classrooms. They are lasting proof of the value of film as both an art form and an educator.

John Ford Festival for the Classroom

DIRECTED BY JOHN FORD, 100 min., color.

This is the American Film Institute's documentary on Ford, and it includes scenes from most of his major films. The problem is that it assumes everybody knows Ford and much of the first reel consists of nostalgic reminiscences about him by John Wayne, James Stewart, and Henry Fonda. Teachers using this might want to show the last reel, which contains the most film clips, first. The film was compiled by Peter Bogdanovich and narrated by Orson Welles.

Rental or lease from Films Inc.

THE INFORMER, 100 min., black and white, 1935.

Ford's Oscar-winning film adaptation of Sean O'Flaherty's

The Man Who Shot Liberty Valance

Films Inc.

famous novella of Irish rebellion. This film holds up quite well, despite its age.
Rental from Films Inc.

JUDGE PRIEST, 80 min., black and white, 1934.
Rental from Films Inc.

THE HURRICANE, 102 min., black and white, 1937.
An excellent film based on the Nordoff and Hall story of bigoted colonial rule in the French East Indies. This film has an amazing storm sequence as its climax. For some strange reason, many film scholars fail to include it among Ford's great works.
Rental from Macmillan Audio Brandon Films.

STAGECOACH, 97 min., black and white, 1939.
Rental from Films Inc.

THE GRAPES OF WRATH, 129 min., black and white, 1940.
Rental from Films Inc.

THE LONG VOYAGE HOME, 105 min., black and white, 1940.
Rental from Films Inc.

SHE WORE A YELLOW RIBBON, 103 min., color, 1948.
Rental from Macmillan Audio Brandon Films.

THE QUIET MAN, 129 min., color, 1952.
Ford's great comedy about an American expatriate in Ireland.
Rental from Ivy Films.

THE SEARCHERS, 119 min., color, 1956.
Rental from Warner Brothers Film Gallery.

THE MAN WHO SHOT LIBERTY VALANCE, 122 min., black and white, 1963.
Rental from Films Inc.

CHEYENNE AUTUMN, 159 min., color, 1964.
Rental from Twyman Films, Swank Films, or Macmillan Audio Brandon Films.

19

The Actor As Teacher— The Teacher As Actor

I conducted the following interview in early 1974 while serving as Films Editor of *Scholastic Teacher* magazine. I am reprinting it here because I feel it has particular relevance for teachers who are interested in the traditional portrayals of their profession in the mass media. At the conclusion I've added a filmography that can be programmed into a unit on Images of the Teacher in Society.

The role of the teacher in the popular media has traditionally been a tour de force for the actors and actresses who've played it. Consider the large number of teacher parts in theater, films, and television that have helped shape the images of the teaching profession in the public eye. Mr. Chips, Miss Dove, Mr. Peepers, Miss Brodie in her prime, Miss Brooks—*Our* Miss Brooks—Mr. Daddy-o Dadier of *The Blackboard Jungle,* Mr. Novak, Annie Sullivan, Blanche Dubois, Sir from *To Sir With Love,* the faculty of *Room 222,* and Mr. Kotter of *Welcome Back Kotter* have provided a varied, sometimes endearing, mostly enduring, portrait of the teacher in society.

While these roles may not always be as realistic and meaningful as those of us in the profession would like, they *are*, at least, dominant roles. Movies and TV shows with teacher parts generally feature them as starring roles. There has developed a whole genre of teacher dramas, which either portray, seriously and comically, the daily tribulations of the classroom (as in *Up the Down Staircase*) or dramatize the life-style of a teacher outside the school (as in *Rachel, Rachel*). Hence the teacher, like the doctor, the private eye, and the cowboy, has become a kind of culture hero. Indeed, quite a few actors and actresses have given their greatest performances in "celluloid classrooms."

When one reviews the variety of teacher portrayals of recent years, it is impossible not to notice the relish with which the performers have taken to these roles. What is there about the role of a teacher that appeals to professional actors? How do these actors adapt themselves to these roles? Do they use real teachers as models for their behavior? Do they identify with teachers? How closely related do they see the two professions—acting and teaching? Are there similar behavioral processes in each? How is the task of an actor performing as a teacher for an audience similar to that of a teacher "performing" for students? Do teachers "act" out their daily roles in the classroom? If they don't, should they?

With questions like these in mind, I spent some time speaking with four distinguished members of the acting profession who have portrayed teachers on the screen. Joanne Woodward, Jon Voight, Sandy Dennis, and John Houseman have each played the role of teacher in a popular film, yet their individual parts were completely different from each other.

Ms. Woodward starred in the 1968 film *Rachel, Rachel* as an over-thirty spinster elementary school teacher.

Although very little of the film dealt with her work in the classroom, the plot did revolve around her problem as an unmarried teacher struggling with the loneliness of small town life.

Jon Voight appeared in a teacher role in the movie *Conrack* (1974). The film, based on the teacher memoir, *The Water Is Wide*, deals with a young, nonconformist named Pat Conroy who takes a job teaching in a middle-elementary school on an isolated island off the coast of Georgia. Conroy (or Conrack as his barely literate students call him) is white, though all his students (indeed, the entire population of the island) are black. In the film Voight projected the sincere, though bungling efforts of the young teacher to work in this environment. In the end he probably has learned as much from his students as he has taught.

John Houseman, the noted theatrical producer and director who was also the Dean of the Drama Division of the Julliard School of Performing Arts in New York, made his screen debut (and won an Oscar) playing a teacher in the 1973 hit film *The Paper Chase*. Houseman portrayed a curmudgeonly and somewhat tyrannical Harvard law professor named Kingsfield whose classroom charisma has a profound effect on one particular student.

Sandy Dennis is perhaps best known to teachers for her portrayal of Sylvia Barrett, the young urban high school English instructor in the film version of *Up the Down Staircase* (1967).

Here is my compilation of the views of these four actor-teachers on their portrayals, their attitudes toward the teaching profession and education in general, and their feelings about what real teachers and actors have in common.

I began the interviews by asking each actor to talk about his or her feelings about playing a teacher on the screen. I asked questions such as: Why did you choose this role? How

Warner Brothers

Rachel, Rachel

qualified did you feel to play it? What insights on teaching did you bring to the role? What teacher, if any, did you model your character after?

Naturally they all made personal references to the characters they portrayed in their films.

JOANNE WOODWARD (referring to *Rachel, Rachel*): I've been around schools a good part of my life. My father was a teacher. He taught in a country school in Thompson, Georgia. It had eleven grades in one building. He later became principal, and he coached football, basketball, and baseball. Eventually he became superintendent of the schools in Blakely, Georgia. So, you see, I've spent an awful lot of time around schools and around schoolteachers.

As for a model for the character of Rachel, I really don't think I chose any particular individual. She was based more on a general impression I had about a certain kind of teacher. When I was in grammar school, there were quite a few of . . . sort of matronly teachers of indeterminate years who always wore faded, well-pressed cottons. I suppose Rachel was rather an old-fashioned teacher in the sense of the elementary teachers I know *now*. Certainly Rachel is not an indication of the modern elementary teacher.

At this point I asked Ms. Woodward if her role as a lonely, small town, old maid contributed to an existing stereotype of teachers.

JOANNE WOODWARD: I suppose that *is* a stereotype to a certain extent. I doubt that it exists now ... that particular stereotype. I mean, the Rachel-types I remember all lived in somebody's house. As a matter of fact, at one time we had a teacher living in our house who had a fairly thankless life, I would imagine, because you had to be absolutely circumspect. And it was confining to be a teacher, particularly an elementary school teacher.

Rachel is really of the past, though not of the past in the sense of when the film took place—the setting was contemporary. She was of the past in the I *saw* her. You know, a woman of another period, living today.

I asked Ms. Woodward if she would ever accept another role as a school teacher or whether she would consider it type casting.

JOANNE WOODWARD (with a smile): Oh, I don't like to play the same kinds of parts over again.

JON VOIGHT (referring to *Conrack*): I wanted to play the part of Pat Conroy because I liked the script. I also enjoyed the book (*The Water is Wide*) and I eventually met the real Pat Conroy, who wrote it, and he impressed me.

. I think that the fact that he was a white person in a black community didn't have anything to do with my wanting to do the script. It was just the idea that he was a teacher and that he was up against some problems. He had a rather flamboyant outlook on life and he obviously had a real desire to help people out, a real joy of life, and a sense of humor, and the story was dramatic enough. It also had a bit of a problem to it, and he had to overcome some things. And it was a love story among people, you know. He falls in love with those kids, they fall in love with him, and in the end they have to go on to other things, and they can't be with each other, and that's a rather sad ending. It was a touching script, and I thought I could make it a touching film.

As far as special research for the role, beyond reading the book and talking to Pat, I didn't really do much. But I've always felt that I could portray a teacher. I've spent a great deal of my life in school, and some teachers had a very strong affect on me. I think the reason I'm an actor today may have been because of one of my high school teachers, Father Bernard McMahon. He taught a course in communications arts at my high school in White Plains (New York). This was a very special class—I'll never forget it. He treated all sorts of communications topics—poetry, speech, theater, film—and he made them alive. I think I remember his class best because he didn't really put any words in our mouths. He opened us all up; he made *our* ideas the focus of the course. And he encouraged us to participate in drama as a form of expression. He directed lots of plays, and he was always attentive to everybody's individual talents. Looking back, I'd have to say that he was one of the best directors I've ever worked with.

At this point I asked if this was the teacher he used as a model for Conrack.

JON VOIGHT: To a certain extent he probably was. But I think, when it comes to relating well with kids, the person who most influenced me, both personally and in my screen role, was my dad. He had passed away just when we began to shoot *Conrack* and after I got over the shock of his loss, I think his personality really influenced my interpretation of the role.

Actually, my dad was a kind of a teacher. He was a golf pro and he taught the sport. He was extremely patient and

Films Inc

Conrack

tolerant of other people. He was also a humorist, a great
kidder and a tease. The zaniness of the Pat Conroy character, his ability to teach kids by playing and joking with them,
was really an extension of my father. My dad believed that
learning should be fun, so did the character in the film, and so
do I.

JOHN HOUSEMAN (referring to his role as the dictatorial
Professor Kingsfield in *The Paper Chase*): The type of teacher
I played is of a very special breed. Kingsfield belongs to a
generation in which charismatic teaching and rather dictatorial teaching were the order of the day. You won't find his
type anymore in high schools, but they still exist in institutions like Harvard, and especially in very specialized studies
such as the law, medicine, and a few others.

    I did some research on this character at Harvard Law

Films Inc.

The Paper Chase

School, and I discovered that he was really a composite of about three or four people on that faculty. You know, professors with somewhat tyrannical reputations who think nothing of subjecting students to rigid and very high standards as well as brutal sarcasm and public put-downs. Yet, I suppose this was their method, and in its own way it did work. It was their way of keeping their own freshness after years and years of teaching the same thing. And, their charismatic, unpredictable, and emotionally violent behavior certainly kept the attention of the students—who would *dare* fall asleep.

I believe that any teacher, no matter what, whom, or where he teaches, is obligated to keep his students aware, interested, and involved. Of course, there are different ways of doing that, and Kingsfield had his own way.

I then asked Mr. Houseman, who has been a college

professor in real life, if he approved of the style of teaching he had portrayed.

JOHN HOUSEMAN: No, but I believe that any teaching method that works is valid. It really depends what you're teaching. In a highly competitive subject like law, the pressure is probably realistic. Here at Julliard Drama School, we try not to make it that competitive, but when you're training actors and putting on shows, even school shows, there is tremendous competition for the best parts. Pressure is part of the process.

I asked him if he personally applied Kingsfield's methods to his students at the Julliard School.

JOHN HOUSEMAN: I do very little actual teaching, though I direct and supervise many plays and handle school admini stration. I would say that I do, as Kingsfield did, refrain from too much personal involvement with my students. Some teachers find they cannot do their jobs, cannot achieve their educational goals, without a certain personal intimacy with students. Others get *too* deeply involved. I remain somewhat aloof. It depends entirely on the individual teacher. I would not recommend any formula for teacher-student relationships.

SANDY DENNIS (referring to her role in *Up the Down Staircase*): To be really honest, I must tell you that I really had no interest in or special knowledge of the teaching profession. The movie studio came to me with a project, and I found it interesting. It wasn't just playing a teacher that was interested me, but I'd enjoyed the book, and I found it humorous. I also was fond of the director.

As for specific preparation for the part, I really didn't have to do much. I've been asked often if I watched other teachers, or did any real teaching, and truthfully I did none of these things. So much of Sylvia Barrett's character is in the script that it really wasn't necessary to go into training. Also, the 50 or so kids who made up my class in the movie were not professional actors, but were given two months of training in improvisational acting before I came on the scene. By the time I arrived to shoot the picture, they had a really swinging thing going as classmates. All I really did was respond to them. Quite a bit in the classroom scenes was improvised, once I got into my character.

I expressed some surprise at Ms. Dennis' comments because her performance was so realistic. I then asked if she at least had some real teacher in mind when she played the part.
SANDY DENNIS: Again, not really. I had one wonderful teacher in junior high school. She was young, and pretty, and sensitive. And she was the one who interested me in drama. But I can't say I had her in mind when I played the part.

In acting you play off other performers' characters. A situation is given to you and the other actors, and then all it really is is imagination. Granted, there are certain parts that you have to do some background work for. For instance, I couldn't play a dancer unless I went into serious training. But playing a teacher—especially this particular teacher—only required that I bring myself to the role. She was a very middle-class, average person, in a very lifelike situation. It wasn't hard to imagine how she would feel and behave.

After the actors had spoken of their feelings about their teacher roles, I then asked each one specifically if he or she could actually be a teacher.
JOANNE WOODWARD: Oh no. I think I'd be a very bad teacher. Teaching requires a special kind of communication of ideas, and the patience one would need to communicate is astounding. I believe in the teachers who teach my children. They have this skill—I don't. I believe in the open classroom, which is part of my children's education, and I know the extraordinary kinds of communicating that goes on in that environment. I'm afraid I personally couldn't provide this kind of teaching myself.

Warner Brothers

Up The Down Staircase

JON VOIGHT: Yes, I think I am a teacher in a way. Acting is a form of communicating. That's teaching.

Also, I've done some real teaching. I taught acting. After I finished *Deliverance*, I went back to acting school because I'd begun to notice some inadequacies in my style. Well, the teacher of the class I enrolled in was a friend of mine, and after it started, he was suddenly, urgently called away. He left me to finish the semester in charge of the class. I hesitated at first, but then it worked out fine. There were 15 of us, and I tried to make it into a cooperative experience. Although as a recognized actor I had a higher status, I didn't want that to interfere. I wanted a classroom of equals, where we would all relate to each other and the various parts we were playing. Eventually, I think, I blended into the group, and we became an assembly of players. I was never the teacher in front of the class giving orders.

I'm glad it worked this way, and I think this kind of teaching would be good for nonacting classes as well. I know a lot of teachers have a power thing with the kids they teach, and it's hard to resist. A teacher can take advantage of the fact that he *knows* what's coming on the next page. But I think this is a potentially dangerous ego problem. I'd like to see more teachers letting their students know that they're just as vulnerable and human as the kids are. That's the kind of teacher I tried to be, and it's the kind that I most approve of.

JOHN HOUSEMAN: I've taught a great deal in the past, but I'm not really a terribly good teacher. I've done a great deal of lecturing, and I run many seminars and all that I do quite well. And around here, I'm the director of the school and I direct plays for them. I don't think I'm patient enough to be a really good teacher.

SANDY DENNIS: I've never had any teacher training or anything like that, but one of my greatest experiences was spending a week at a college recently teaching acting. I enjoyed it tremendously, and I think after that experience that I would want to teach acting more often. My problem is that my work in theater and films causes me to travel too often to establish any kind of teaching base. Still it's great to teach, especially from an acting point of view. It helps to reinterest you in something, and it stimulates your imagination. I also am fascinated in dealing with the individual members of a class and helping develop their individual talents. It's very rewarding, and I guess this is how most teachers must feel.

My next question to each actor was, Do you see any similarities between the processes of acting and teaching? Are teachers in a sense actors, and vice versa?

JOANNE WOODWARD: I don't think teaching and acting are so similar at all. At least, I don't believe they should be. Acting is role playing; by its very nature it's insincere. Teaching must be totally honest, totally sincere. I realize that in many schools where teachers must teach the same subjects period after period, day after day, that they probably must role play in order to survive and keep going. I'm sure these pressures faced my father. But ideally, again, citing the open class-room philosophy, I don't think acting will make for better teaching.

JON VOIGHT: I think there are similarities between teachers and actors. Teachers explain things, they tell stories, they illustrate. In a sense they are dramatizing their lessons to make them more meaningful and memorable to kids. I think there's a bit of the actor in all good teachers. And, as I've said, acting and teaching are both personal forms of communication.

Something I'd like to add here is that a teacher is sometimes a director, in the theatrical sense, as well as an actor. In the classroom often the kids are the actors and the teacher directs them. Sometimes he must be the performer, and sometimes he has to appreciate and guide the performances of others. In that sense, there are analogies between the theater and the classroom.

JOHN HOUSEMAN: Beyond certain obvious similarities, I don't know. To a certain extent all behavior is acting, role playing. There have been volumes written on the psychology of these things, and we all know them. As I've said, I think it is a great benefit for teachers to have certain charismatic qualities, and these are certainly beneficial to actors too. In that sense, I suppose there are similarities.

SANDY DENNIS: There are some similarities between daily teaching the same subject and stage acting. When you're in a play that runs for, say, a year, and you have to recite the same lines night after night, you need to constantly remotivate yourself to escape the boredom. I imagine it's the same in teaching. But when you've got a good audience—and you can sense this after a few minutes—and they're involved in your performance, you're not bored, and no matter how many times you've played the part, it's exciting again. I would hope that's how a teacher reacts to an interested class.

On the other hand, though, acting is only pretending, and this can create problems for teachers. I mean, if you get angry you should show anger. I think kids would see through your pretense and think you are dishonest. And I think teaching should be based on honest relationships between teachers and students. In that sense, it's not like acting at all.

I concluded each interview by asking if some kind of dramatic training might be beneficial for teachers. Could we be better teachers by mastering some of the techniques of acting?
JOANNE WOODWARD: Definitely not.
JON VOIGHT: I think it might be good for teachers to observe some drama classes, particularly noting the relationship between the actors and the director. Also acting teaches you to better know yourself. And, since acting is a cooperative art, drama training helps people relate better to each other. I think anybody, not just teachers, could benefit from this.

Still, a good teacher is involved in more subtle kind of performing and much deeper personal relationships. In that sense, his is a much greater art.
JOHN HOUSEMAN: There's no general rule here. I think all teachers need training in public speaking and address. I mean if a teacher is shy and timid and had trouble facing an audience, his job would certainly be more difficult. But as for specific training in the dramatic arts, I really don't know. Perhaps for some individuals . . .
SANDY DENNIS: I don't think so. If I could require anything for teachers, it would be training in adolescent psychology and group dynamics. I can't see how acting lessons would substitute for these. Teaching is so much more than acting.

Filmography

RACHEL, RACHEL, 104 min., color, 1968.
Rental from Twyman Films or Swank Films. Note: This film has numerous other uses besides this context—particularly a unit on Women's Studies, see chapter 13.

UP THE DOWN STAIRCASE, 123 min., color, 1968.
Rental from Twyman Films, Swank Films, or Macmillan Audio Brandon Films. Complete screenplay available in the *Identity* volume of Scholastic's "Literature of the Screen" series.

THE PAPER CHASE, 110 min., color, 1973.
Rental from Films Inc.

CONRACK, 114 min., color, 1974.
Rental from Films Inc.

THE BLACKBOARD JUNGLE, 101 min., black and white, 1955.
A blistering portrait of an urban ghetto school, which became a prototype film about education. Despite its negative images, this is still a very powerful movie.
Rental from Films Inc.

GOOD MORNING MISS DOVE, 100 min., color, 1954.
A typical goody-goody view of the self-sacrificing old maid schoolteacher who changed the lives of her students. Nauseating, but definitely a stereotype worth examining.
Rental from Films Inc.

THE PRIME OF MISS JEAN BRODIE, 116 min., color, 1969.
A British film about a self-deluded, self-centered, neo-fascist teacher and her influence on her students in a girls boarding school. Maggie Smith in her Oscar-winning portrayal is a nice antidote to Miss Dove.
Rental from Films Inc.

TO SIR WITH LOVE, 105 min., color, 1967.
Sidney Poitier as super teacher in a London slum school. A new kind of stereotype.
Rental from Twyman Films or Swank Films.

THE MIRACLE WORKER, 107 min., black and white, 1962.
Brilliant film of William Gibson's play about Annie Sullivan, Helen Keller's famous tutor.
Rental from United Artists 16.

Appendices

Filmography—
100 More Titles

In an effort to be as comprehensive as possible, I am adding an additional 100 titles of films that may be useful to teachers in any number of contexts not covered in this book.

THE ADVENTURES OF ROBINSON CRUSOE, 102 min., color, 1952.

A brilliant film of Defoe's classic survival novel, directed by, of all people, the great surrealist filmmaker Luis Bunuel. The film has a good straightforward narrative flow, using much of Defoe's prose in Crusoe's off-screen narration. In addition, the performance of Dan O'Herlihy in the title role skillfully captures the feelings of loneliness and psychological hardship of life in isolation. This film was out of circulation for a number of years, and it is certainly good to have it available for classrooms again.

Rental from Macmillan Audio Brandon Films.

ALL QUIET ON THE WESTERN FRONT, 105 min., black and white, 1930.

For me this has always been the most powerful of all anti-war films. Despite its age and the dated ring of some of the dialogue, this sad and humane portrait of young German soldiers in the waning days of World War I never fails to move students. The film would work well in units on twentieth-century history for its accurate portrayal of World War I trench warfare. It can also be used effectively in a cross-media study with Erich Maria Remarque's novel.

Rental from Universal 16.

ALL THE PRESIDENT'S MEN, 148 min., color, 1976.

The best movie about American journalism ever made. This extremely popular film version of the Woodward-Bernstein Watergate exposé is a fascinating view of the process of investigative reporting. Journalists at work—on the phone, pounding the pavement, interviewing source after source, checking details, cross-checking, verifying, re-verifying—is what the film is really about. The fact that these journalists are uncovering the political scandal of the century creates a sense of dramatic urgency, but the film's lasting power is in its demonstration of the operation of a free press. I imagine the film, and the book on which it is based, will become staples in many high school and college journalism courses.

All The President's Men

Warner Brothers

A footnote in the history of screen censorship is that the MPAA ultimately rated *All the President's Men* P.G., despite certain taboo four-letter words that had previously been grounds for "R" ratings. This has meant a slight revision of the MPAA's unofficial standards. Normally I deplore profanity in films (as I've indicated throughout these pages), but in this case the language is not gratuitous. Considering the historical implications of the Watergate story, it would have been a shame for a realistic movie about it to have it's explitives deleted.

Rental from Warner Brothers Film Gallery.

AMERICAN GRAFFITI, 110 min., color, 1973.

One of 1970s box office sensations and, for me, the best movie in a long, long time. On the surface, *American Graffiti* is a relatively plotless film about one night in the lives of four teen-age boys in a small California town. It takes place in 1962 and is saturated with vintage rock music of the '50s and early '60s. From that brief synopsis and the film's awful promotion—"Where were you in '62?"—*American Graffiti* may seem like a sentimental bit of nostalgia. Actually, it is a superbly made portrait of the end of an era, a somewhat innocent era, before Vietnam, assassinations, drug culture, student protests, and Watergate. The film is also a marvelous example of expert filmmaking, brilliantly edited to tell the four interrelated stories of its major characters. The director, George Lucas, is probably the most talented young filmmaker in the United States, and *Graffiti* can be shown in classrooms as a text on style and technique.

Rental from Universal 16.

THE ANGEL LEVINE, 114 min., color, 1970.

For some reason this excellent film of a Bernard Malamud story has never been popular, theatrically or in the classroom. Normally fantasies about angels returning to earth turn me off too, but this beautiful fable about a black Jewish angel named Levine (Harry Belefonte) who tries to restore faith to a destitute old tailor (Zero Mostel) is extremely moving. It is also a thinly disguised tract on contemporary black-Jewish relations and a moving plea for universal tolerance. Directed by Czech filmmaker Jan Kadar.

Rental from United Artists 16.

ATTACK, 107 min., black and white, 1956.

This is one of the most powerful films I have ever used with high school students, but it is not for the squeamish. *Attack* is an anti-war film about a World War II company of soldiers under the command of a captain who is a psychopathic coward. It deals with the efforts of the men to cope with this officer and the politics of the military establishment, which covers up the captain's incompetance so as not to create any embarrassing incidents. Directed by the highly competent Robert Aldrich and starring Jack Palance, Eddie Albert, and Lee Marvin, this film is an excellent vehicle for dealing with issues involving human values and ethics. It can be used in the same context as a film such as *Paths of Glory*, but *Attack* rents for a lot less money.

Rental from United Artists 16.

THE AUTOBIOGRAPHY OF MISS JANE PITTMAN, 110 min., color, 1974.

This is probably the best made-for-television movie yet. Cicely Tyson stars in an almost 100-year odyssey of a black woman in the American South. Miss Jane Pittman begins life as a slave and subsequently becomes a pioneer, a businesswoman, a community leader, and a modern civil rights activist. The film is a little too long (TV movies traditionally equate length to importance) but would be an excellent source in a black history or women's studies unit.

Rental or lease from Learning Corporation of America.

BAD COMPANY, 92 min., color, 1973.

A lively, exciting, and relevant screen portrait of a group of young draft resisters during the Civil War. The boys go West to escape the Union conscriptionists, only to find a different kind of survival struggle on the Great Plains. Splendid acting, particularly by Jeff Bridges. Written and directed by the team of Benton and Newman who wrote *Bonnie and Clyde*.

Rental from Films Inc.

BAD DAY AT BLACK ROCK, 81 min., color, 1955.

A classic film with real teaching potential. Spencer Tracy stars as a one-armed World War II veteran who visits a small desert town to deliver a posthumous medal won by a Japanese-American

Films Inc.

Bad Company

soldier. Tracy searches for the soldier's father but meets a web of resistance and bigotry. This film is both an engrossing suspense drama and a provocative study of mob psychology and intolerance. Highly recommended.

Rental from Films Inc.

BASIC FILM TERMS, 20 min., color, 1973.

One of a series of how-to-do-it films, this lovely short cleverly demonstrates 20 or so key concepts in moviemaking—zoom, cut, track, pan, dolly, wipe, and so on. A good introductory source for a filmmaking class, though others in the series—particularly the film on special effects—are rather superficial.

Rental or purchase from Pyramid Films.

THE BIG CARNIVAL (original title, *Ace in a Hole*), 112 min., black and white, 1951.

A superb, if somewhat depressing film about the sensationalistic press in the United States. An unscrupulous newspaperman (Kirk Douglas) tries to capitalize on the plight of a man trapped in a mine cave-in by prolonging the rescue, ultimately causing the man's death. Nicely directed and scripted by Billy Wilder, the film is particularly relevant for "detached" Americans.

Rental from Films Inc.

A BIG HAND FOR THE LITTLE LADY, 95 min., color, 1965.

A very entertaining film, adapted from a TV play about a group of wealthy poker players in the old West getting "conned" out of their bankrolls. It is a masterpiece of its genre, and whenever people tout *The Sting*, I refer them to this classy little comedy. Features a superb cast (and a marvelous example of repertory playing for a drama class), including Joanne Woodward, Henry Fonda, Jason Robards, Paul Ford, and Kevin McCarthy.

Rental from Twyman Films or Swank Films.

BLOW-UP, 108 min., color, 1967.

Michelangelo Antonnione's cryptic film about "mod" London was a huge success in the '60s and holds up quite well today. A callous, young photographer snaps a picture of a pretty woman in a park, only to discover upon blowing it up that he's witnessed a murder. The photographer's moral dilemma, and his ultimate inability to act, raise some challenging issues for a personal values discussion. The director's constant use of symbolism, pretentious by some standards, may make for some interesting classroom analysis. *Blow-Up* has some snatches of female nudity, which made it controversial in its time (though harmless by today's standards), so it would be a good idea to secure administrative and community clearance before showing it.

Rental from Films Inc.

BONNIE AND CLYDE, 111 min., color, 1967.

One of the most influential films of the past 20 years, Arthur Penn's *Bonnie and Clyde* is generally regarded as a definitive gangster-as-tragic hero film. Actually, the movie would be of most interest to classes in film history and/or aesthetics, since its script is basically an extension of the adult western.

Rental from MacMillan Audio Brandon Films, Twyman Films, or Swank Films.

CITIZEN KANE, 119 min., black and white, 1940.

Quite possibly the best American film of all time, Orson Wells' *Citizen Kane* is a loose biography of William Randolph Hearst, plus a lot more. It can be studied for its fascinating portrait of a power-hungry publisher or analyzed for its innovative cinematic techniques. Teachers using it should also refer to Pauline

Kael's fascinating, if not always accurate, *Citizen Kane Book* (Bantam, 1974), which also includes the complete script.

Rental or long-term lease from Films Inc. Check regional libraries for free loan.

CLAUDINE, 105 min., color, 1974.

During the early '70s Hollywood discovered the black movie audience and produced a whole flood of generally mediocre "blaxexploitation" films, full of racism, violence, and sex. By 1975 the popularity of such trash as *Superfly, Blacula, Trouble Man, Hit Man, The Legend of Nigger Charlie*, and the like declined sharply. In the midst of this barrage of junk, however, one genuinely fine black film did emerge, portraying urban life on its own realistic, tragic-comic terms. *Claudine* is a story of a pretty, husbandless woman with a brood of kids to support. She's on welfare, working on the sly as a domestic to pick up some extra cash, only to be threatened with losing her welfare benefits when her job is discovered by a case worker. In addition, she is in love with a man whom she'd like to marry, but who earns less than her welfare benefits. The film is an often funny satire on the welfare system and a moving portrait of black Americans. Starring Dianne Carroll (cast against type and excellent) and James Earl Jones.

Rental from Films Inc.

THE CLOWNS, 90 min., color, 1973. (In Italian; English subtitles; dubbed print available upon request.)

A loving tribute to circus life by the great Italian director, Federico Fellini. This film is particularly interesting in the pseudo-documentary style Fellini employs. All of its footage is staged; some with actors, some with real circus people, but all controlled and scripted. This would be an excellent source for a filmmaking course.

Rental from Films Inc.

THE CONVERSATION, 101 min., color, 1974.

Francis Ford Coppola's brilliant, frightening movie about the gradual breakdown of a wiretapper was the definitive film of the Watergate era. This film works on two levels: as a chilling suspense tale, and as a commentary on the dangerous loss of privacy in contemporary society. Superbly acted by Gene Hackman as the wire-

Films Inc.

The Conversation

tapper, John Cazale as his assistant, and Allen Garfield as an up-in'-coming "bugging" expert.

Rental from Films Inc.

THE CROWD, 100 min., silent, 1927.

A classic film of the late silent era, directed and scripted by King Vidor. *The Crowd* is a moving, tragic tale of the dehumanizing affects of urban life on a young worker and his wife. Some of the sequences depicting the man at his excessively routinized office job provide a powerful commentary on the American society of the twenties.

Rental from Films Inc.

DAY FOR NIGHT, 110 min., color, 1974. (In French; English subtitles; dubbed print available on request.)

Francois Truffaut's lovingly made tribute to the world's moviemakers. This alternately funny and sad film about the making of a movie is an entertaining behind-the-scenes tour de force. It can be used as a virtual filmmaking textbook. Truffaut, incidentally, plays one of the starring roles, typecast as the director.

Rental from Warner Brothers Film Gallery.

DEAD BIRDS, 90 min., color, 1963.

A fascinating documentary, produced by Harvard's Peabody

Anthropological Museum, about the warlike Dani culture of New Guinea. It would be an excellent source for high school or college anthropology or sociology classes. It is also a superb example of objective documentary filmmaking.

Purchase or rental from Phoenix Films.

DEADLINE U.S.A., 95 min., black and white, 1952.

A very realistic portrait of the modern newspaper world. Humphrey Bogart portrays an editor of a big city daily on the verge of bankruptcy. The film has a lot to say about the day-to-day operation of a newspaper and would be a valuable source for a journalism class. Written and directed by Richard Brooks.

Rental from Films Inc.

DESPERATE CHARACTERS, 90 min., color, 1972.

This is a sad, overly pessimistic portrait of modern urban life, written and directed by noted playwright Frank D. Gilroy. Shirley MacLaine portrays an affluent New York housewife who is victimized by a callous husband, vandals, a mugger, and a (possibly) rabid cat. If all this sounds particularly depressing, it is, but the film is cautiously recommended because it represents a rather unique effort to create a kind dirgelike cinematic poem. Please don't try to use it as a realistic representation of urban life.

Rental from Films Inc.

THE DO-IT-YOURSELF CARTOON KIT, 6 min., color, 1962.

A wild, hilarious British animated film by Bob Godfrey. Teachers looking for a source to illustrate various animation techniques will find this film particularly valuable.

Purchase or rental from Pyramid Films.

DIVORCE AMERICAN STYLE, 109 min., color, 1967.

The team of Bud Yorkin and Norman Lear is currently the hottest source of American TV comedy (*All in the Family, Maude,* and *Sanford and Son*). Their films also reflect the sharp sting of meaningful social satire. *Divorce American Style*, a spoof on current divorce laws, is a good example of the effective use of humor to examine a serious social issue. Despite its antiseptic cast (Dick Van Dyke, Debbie Reynolds, Van Johnson), this film is an extremely potent adult comedy. It can be useful in a unit or elective on human sexuality and marriage. Because of its mature content, it is not recommended for junior high students.

Rental from Macmillan Audio Brandon Films, Twyman Films, or Swank Films.

DUCK SOUP, 80 min., black and white, 1933.

The best of all the Marx Brothers movies, this has the advantage of also being *about something. Duck Soup* is a hysterical assault on militarism in the 1930s, full of barbed asides at the petty nationalism in Eastern Europe. The opening anthem "Hail Freedonia," as sung by the inimitable Groucho, may be the funniest song in movie history.

Rental from Universal 16 as are such other Marx Brothers classics as *Horse Feathers, Monkey Business, Coconuts,* and *Animal Crackers.*

THE EMPEROR JONES, 80 min., black and white, 1933.

For many years this strange and remarkable film was lost and only recently, thanks to an American Film Institute grant, has most of the footage been restored. (The old nitrate negative had almost totally deteriorated, a problem accounting for the disappearance of many older films.) The great, controversial Paul Robeson skillfully portrayed Eugene O'Neill's black potentate. Despite the pseudo-Othello overtones of the plot, this classic is worth seeing for Robeson's defiance of the traditional black stereotype found in films of the '30s and for some revolutionary cinematography, including several full close-ups of the black actor. (In those days even the camera used to discriminate against black actors.)

Rental from Images, Inc.

THE FABLE OF HE AND SHE, 16 min., color, 1975.

Delightful film of clay animated figures by Eliot Noyes, Jr. A mythological land, where sex roles in the society of mushamels (women) and harbybars (men) are fixed, is suddenly split in half, forcing each sex to master the other's roles as well as its own. When their island is joined together again, some important lessons have been learned. This is one of the few films I have seen that can work effectively with both the youngest and oldest of students.

Purchase or rental from Learning Corporation of America.

The Fixer

THE FAMILY WAY, 115 min., color, 1967.

A wonderful British film adapted from Bill Naughton's play *All in Good Time* about a young couple who can't consummate their marriage. The couple (Hywell Bennett and Haley Mills) are forced by a housing shortage to live in the boy's parents' house, where privacy is at a premium. They've also been cheated out of their honeymoon by a crooked travel agent, getting their marriage off on a definite wrong foot. The whole situation is treated in human, comic terms, and they eventually work out their initial domestic problems. Despite its adult theme, this film is extremely tasteful in its approach and would be an excellent source in a high school values course. The complete script is available in the *Men and Women* volume of Scholastic's "Literature of the Screen" Series.

Rental of the film from Twyman Films.

FELLINI: A DIRECTOR'S NOTEBOOK, 90 min., color, 1970.

A valuable documentary on the work of Italian master Federico Fellini. The film traces his career and his art (with a few scenes from his best films) and also follows him as he directs the film *Satyricon*. A useful source in a film aesthetics or filmmaking course.

Rental from Films Inc.

THE FIXER, 132 min., color, 1968.

A powerful film of Bernard Malamud's famous novel about a Jew wrongly accused of ritual murder in Czarist Russia. Based on a true incident, the film is at its best in portraying the harsh life in ghettos at that time. (There is one powerful sequence of cossack troops charging defenseless Jews during one of the infamous pogroms of the late 19th century.) The major emphasis of the plot is on the young agnostic Jew who is tried for murder and how he becomes a faithful believer in God as a result of his persecution. It is in this area that the script occasionally borders on melodrama, with good and evil so well defined that they become stereotyped. Still, this could be a valuable classroom source.

Rental from Films Inc.

FORBIDDEN GAMES, 90 min., black and white, 1952. (In French; English subtitles.)

A classic French film about the impact of war on the lives of two small children. An orphaned girl and her boy playmate watch the ritual of burials in their village during World War II. Soon they begin to play a game of burying dead animals and marking their graves with ornaments they steal from the village church. The adults of the town discover the "games" and ironically punish the children. *Forbidden Games* is a powerful anti-war film and represents one of the finest achievements in French cinema. Directed by René Clement.

Rental from Macmillan Audio Brandon Films.

FRANK FILM, 8 min., color, 1974.

An Oscar-winning animated film, artfully composed of hundreds of images and sounds depicting the autobiography of its maker—Frank Morris. This film is particularly interesting for its highly complex overlapping soundtrack (produced by sound expert Tony Schwartz), which literally provides two narratives at once.

Purchase or rental from Pyramid Films.

FREUD: THE HIDDEN NATURE OF MAN, 27 min., color, 1971.

One of the few made-for-the-classroom films that I've ever found useful. This is a dramatized documentary about some of Freud's initial psychoanalytic breakthroughs. Some of its techniques include an actor playing Freud as an on-screen narrator and a vivid dramatization of the id, ego, super ego struggle within the individual.

Purchase or rental from Learning Corporation of America.

THE FRONT PAGE, 110 min., color, 1974.

I suppose I am biased toward this particular version of the Hecht-MacArthur newspaper play, since I spent a week on the set watching Billy Wilder shoot it. The film was not particularly well received, but it's very funny, and the dialogue is updated just enough to give it a very contemporary sting. The excellent cast features Jack Lemmon as an older version of Hildy Johnson, Walter Matthau as the meanest Walter Burns ever, and a bunch of great repertory actors as the reporters—David Wayne, Allen Garfield, Charles Dunning, Dick O'Niell, and Herb Edelman. Only

Front Page (1974 version)

Universal

Carol Burnett, miscast as the "notorious Molly Mallory," is ineffective.

Rental from Universal 16.

THE GENERAL, 90 min., silent, 1926.

The great Buster Keaton's most memorable film. *The General* is about a meek little locomotive engineer who heroically captures a Confederate train for the Union army. A memorable film and a technically excellent one.

Rental from Macmillan Audio Brandon Films.

GO ASK ALICE, 82 min., color, 1972.

A very well made TV movie (directed by John Korty) of the tragic anonymous diary of a young girl who ultimately destroyed herself with drugs. Though the film glosses over some of the horrors of the book, it can be used as an effective tool in drug education programs.

Rental from Twyman Films or Swank Films.

THE GOLDEN FISH, 20 min., color, 1959.

Beautifully made French film by Edmond Sechan about a pet canary and a goldfish, and the alley cat who almost does away with both. The film is simply done, but the climactic scene in which the cat actually puts the fish back in its bowl is astounding. Excellent for elementary classes.

Purchase or rental from Learning Corporation of America.

GREED, 114 min., silent, 1923.

This is a legendary silent film by the extravagant director Erich Von Stroheim and was brutally cut down from its original six-hour length when released. Based on Frank Norris' rugged novel *McTeague*, the film is chaotic and often incoherent due to the cutting, but fascinating to watch nevertheless. This is particularly true of the climax, which was filmed on location in the sweltering heat of Death Valley. Of particular interest to film history students.

Rental from Films Inc.

THE GROUNDSTAR CONSPIRACY, 96 min., color, 1972.

This film can probably best be described as the first Watergate era movie, though it received little recognition in its initial theatrical release. George Peppard portrays a callous CIA-type agent called Tuxan, who sets out to discover the identity of the saboteurs who destroyed "Groundstar," a government computer center. His methods, however, which include the creation of a drug-induced human robot to infiltrate the spy ring, and his uncanny expertise at invading the privacy of the innocent as well as the guilty make him as dangerous as the enemy he pursues. A meaningful, thought-provoking thriller.

Rental from Universal 16 or Twyman Films.

HAIL THE CONQUERING HERO, 100 min., black and white, 1944.

A very funny satire on some sacred American institutions, including heroism, small town life, politics, and even motherhood. Written and directed by the greatest screen satirist of the 30s and 40s, Preston Sturges, the film traces adventures of Woodrow Wilson Pershing Truesmith (Eddie Bracken), who is drummed out of the army because of severe hay fever. His army buddies decide to bring him back to his home town as a decorated war hero, and as a result of the hoax, he becomes the town's mayor. Despite the age of this film, it still works very well with today's students.

Rental from Universal 16.

THE HAUNTING, 112 min., black and white, 1963.

A brilliantly made, gimmick-free gothic thriller based on Shirley Jackson's novel *The Haunting of Hill House*. There are two excellent performances by Julie Harris and Claire Bloom and fine direction by the usually uneven Robert Wise. (He's done fine work—*The Set-Up, I Want to Live, The Sandpebbles*—and sloppy stuff—*Star* and *Hindenburg*.) This is a particularly good film for a unit on gothic-horror literature, with readings from Hawthorne, Poe, and Daphne du Maurier.

Rental from Films Inc.

HESTER STREET, 95 min., black and white, 1975.

A little gem of a movie, directed by a fairly inexperienced woman named Joan Micklin Silver (whose career now demands to be watched closely). The film traces the lives of some Eastern European Jewish immigrants living on New York's Lower East Side in the late 1880s. It is particularly effective in dealing with the tribulations of a young wife (Carol Kane) who has joined her husband in America after remaining behind in Europe for two years. The husband has become "a regular Yankee," seeing himself as an assimilated American, complete with a girl friend on the side. The wife's rude awakening to American society and her ultimate liberation (a highlight of the film is a Hebrew divorce ceremony) are alternately sad and funny. This is really a one-of-a-kind movie—a very realistic depiction of immigrant life and a timely tract on women's lib.

Rental from Cinema V.

THE HILL, 122 min., black and white, 1965.

A tough, British-made film about a military prison for nonconformist soldiers during World War II. A tough sergeant prides himself on his record of being able to recondition men for combat in 30 days by forcing them to continuously assault a 30-foot sand hill. This film has much to say about the nature of power and society's intolerance of deviant behavior. It features some excellent performances by Sean Connery as a resistant prisoner, Harry Andrews as the sergeant, and Ossie Davis as a black recruit who rebels against military racism. Teachers should be cautioned about the film's dialogue, however, since much of it is in garbled British-cockney slang, making it difficult for students to understand every word. Still, the film has enough solid content to make it worthwhile in spite of this seeming flaw.

Rental from Films Inc.

HIGH NOON, 85 min., black and white, 1952.

This famous morality play in the form of a western still ranks among my favorite classroom films. Marshall Will Kane's lone stand against a group of cutthroats, while the townspeople meekly stand by, is a powerful allegory on corruption and violence in American society. Screenwriter Carl Foreman (who was blacklisted for his political views soon after the film came out) claims to have been really portraying the McCarthyist America of the early fifties, though curiously many of the film's statements on "law and order" seem very reactionary by today's standards. *High Noon* is also an important film from a cinematic viewpoint, since it is brilliantly edited, and is one of the few movies that successfully simulates "real time"—it runs 85 minutes and treats 85 minutes of action. Complete screenplay available in Scholastic's "Literature of the Screen" series in the volume called *Values in Conflict*.

Rental from Ivy Films. (I should note that for a long time *High Noon* was available from many distributors at a very low price. Now Ivy has exclusive domain over it and rents it at a considerably higher rate. Teachers have written and told me that they feel the great price increase is unfair and have begun to look for alternative films.)

THE HIRELING, 102 min., color, 1973.

This excellent British film of L.P. Hartley's '20s novel won a prize at the Cannes Film Festival, yet it received a very limited American distribution. It is a seething critique of the British social class system and is directed in the unpretentious, realistic style of such acclaimed films as *Room at the Top* and *Saturday Night and Sunday Morning*. Its story of a working class chauffeur who helps an aristocratic young woman through a time of strife and then falls in love with her could be remote and irrelevant to many students. However, the chauffeur's plight—he is ignored by the lady, since he is of a "lower station"—is superbly portrayed. Actor Robert Shaw portrays the rejected chauffeur with the proper combination of compassion, bewilderment, and raging anger. Students are bound to be moved by this film, which can generate a good deal of discussion and creative writing.

Rental from Columbia Cinematheque.

HIS GIRL FRIDAY, 95 min., black and white, 1941.

A very funny version of *The Front Page*, adapted for the screen by Ben Hecht and Charles MacArthur, the original playwrights. In this "edition" Hildy Johnson is "Hilda" Johnson, worldly woman reporter, played by Rosalind Russell. Cary Grant portrays the cantankerous editor Walter Burns with considerably more charm than a character like that deserves. Directed by the efficient Hollywood pro Howard Hawks.

Rental from Macmillan Audio Brandon Films.

HOA BINH, 102 min., color, 1970. (In French and Vietnamese; English subtitles.)

Although nominated for an Academy Award and universally

Transvue Pictures

Hoa-Binh

acclaimed by critics, this superb film about a small boy and his sister's courageous odyssey through war-torn Saigon did virtually no business when released in the United States. The film is non-political—the North and South Vietnamese are both the enemies to these struggling children—and I suppose advocates of both American withdrawal and commitment were turned off by that. *Hoa Binh* (Vietnamese for peace), however, is a genuine masterpiece in the tradition of *Forbidden Games* and deserves a large audience. Directed by the excellent French cinematographer Raol Coutard.

To date there is no 16mm distributor for this film. A pity.

THE HOODLUM PRIEST, 101 min., black and white, 1961.

This is a good film to use in a unit on criminology and law enforcement. Based on the true story of a Jesuit priest, Charles Dismas Clark, it depicts the role of religion as a factor in the rehabilitation of criminals. The film pulls few punches and raises many issues for discussion, including the controversial "tough guy" attitude of the young priest. Actor Don Murray is extremely good as Father Clark, and Keir Dullea (later to achieve acclaim in *David and Lisa*) made his screen debut as a delinquent youth. I was surprised to learn that this film is not shown much in secondary schools; it's a classroom natural.

Rental from United Artists 16.

HUD, 112 min., black and white, 1963.

Powerful modern western, with Paul Newman in the anti-hero title role. This film is based on an early novel by Larry McMurtry —*Horsemen, Pass By*—and is a very realistic portrait of the stark, boring existence of the "Cadillac" cowboy in today's rural West. There is an excellent analytical review of this film which might make a useful student resource by Pauline Kael in her book *I Lost It at the Movies* (Little, Brown, 1965).

Rental from Films Inc.

INTRUDER IN THE DUST, 87 min., black and white, 1947.

A very fine adaptation of the difficult-to-read William Faulkner novel (screenplay by Ben Maddow, directed by Clarence Brown). The film depicts the act of conscience of a teen-age white boy who works to prove an old black man innocent of a murder accusation in rural, racist Mississippi. The dialogue is very close to Faulkner's text, and the entire film is very much in keeping with the spirit of the novel. It is also noteworthy for its depiction of the black prisoner, Lucas Beauchamp (Juano Hernandez) as a fierce individualist, in contrast to black stereotypes common on the screen in the 30s and 40s.

Rental from Films Inc.

ITALIANAMERICAN, 48 min., color, 1974.

A delightful nonfiction film about second generation life in an Italian-American household. Noted director Martin Scorcese (*Mean Streets, Alice Doesn't Live Here Anymore, Taxi Driver*) made a film of his parents' reminiscences about life in New York's "Little Italy." Mr. and Mrs. Scorcese are on screen much of the time in their living room describing life as it was "in the old days." This is one of the few oral history films ever made, and it is a loving tribute to a passing way of life. Produced under a grant from the National Endowment for the Arts.

No 16mm distributor yet. Watch for it.

KING KONG, 100 min., black and white, 1933.

You can't keep a good man down! Despite the remakes, nothing in Hollywood history will ever surpass the technical miracles in this early horror-fantasy epic. In a classroom setting the film is also interesting for its unconscious commentary on American attitudes toward urban life, symbolized by the great ape's tumultuous revenge on the city of New York. A true agrarian Jeffersonian that Kong.

Rental from Films Inc. or Janus Films. Check local libraries for free loan.

LARRY, 78 min., color, 1974.

Originally made for television, this is a deeply moving film about a young man raised in a mental institution who actually had normal intelligence. Based on a true story, this is an excellent source for a classroom unit on psychology. Brilliantly acted by Frederick Forrest in the title role.

Purchase, lease or rental from Learning Corporation of America.

LITTLE BIG MAN, 160 min., color, 1970.

Overlong and uneven, but still one of the greatest of all western films. Arthur Penn's direction, Calder Willingham's adaptation of the Thomas Berger novel, and Dustin Hoffman's performance of the symbolic "everyman" Jack Crabbe, all make this film the event that it is. Highly recommended for units in United States history, particularly those examining the extermination of the Plains Indians.

Rental from Swank Films.

LORD OF THE FLIES, 90 min., black and white, 1963.

Peter Brook's fine British film of William Golding's famous allegorical novel about a desert island society run by boys. This film would work particularly well with unmotivated students or poor readers who might otherwise never be exposed to the book.

Rental from Twyman Films.

MADAME BOVARY, 127 min., black and white, 1948.

This flawed Hollywood version of Flaubert's great novel of a country wife's infidelities is recommended because of its thematic

Little Big Man

relevance. I don't know if all teachers can teach the novel in high school, but the somewhat cleaned-up movie version certainly shouldn't present any censorship problems. It also includes a fascinating prologue dealing with Flaubert (well played by James Mason) being put on trial for obscenity and citing the universality of Emma Bovary's plight among all women. The film's major weakness is in the casting of whiny Jennifer Jones as Emma, though the supporting cast and the direction of Vincent Minnelli are good. This is one classic that might benefit from an intelligent remake.

Rental from Films Inc.

THE MANCHURIAN CANDIDATE, 126 min., black and white, 1962.

A political thriller-fantasy for all time. A group of American prisoners are brainwashed in Korea, and one is programmed to become a political assassin. The complex plot also involves the assassin's politically ambitious mother who is a Communist double agent married to a right-wing Senator. A fascinating commentary on modern psychology and politics. Directed by John Frankenheimer, and scripted by George Axelrod, from Richard Condon's novel.

Rental from United Artists 16.

MEDIUM COOL, 110 min., color, 1969.

Along with *Easy Rider* (which is not acceptable classroom fare), this film is perhaps the best movie document of the late 60s. Director Haskell Wexler created a fictional story about a rather callous TV camera-man (much like the photographer in *Blow-Up*) who gradually becomes sensitized to the traumas in American society in the late 60s. Much of the footage in the film was shot during the explosive demonstrations in Chicago at the site of the controversial 1968 Democratic national convention. The film is flawed—a pretentious nude scene got it an X rating in 1969, though this was later lowered to an R—but is a must for students of recent American history.

Rental from Films Inc.

MY SWEET CHARLIE, 96 min., color, 1970.

One of the first really good movies made for television, *My Sweet Charlie* is a slightly dated but touching drama about a relationship between a white, pregnant, runaway teen-ager and a fugitive black civil rights worker who are forced to hide together in an abandoned summer house. The film is well acted by Patty Duke and Al Freeman, Jr., and is a good object lesson in human understanding.

Rental from Universal 16.

NOSFERATU, 85 min., black and white, silent, 1922.

The definitive version of Bram Stoker's *Dracula*, directed by one of the great filmmakers of all time, F.W. Murnau. This is an excellent source for courses in cinema history.

Rental from Macmillan Audio Brandon Films or the Museum of Modern Art.

THE NUTTY PROFESSOR, 107 min., color, 1963.

French film critics generally regard Jerry Lewis as one of the great screen comedians and filmmakers, in the tradition of Keaton and Chaplin. I have never been able to understand their zealous defense of him, with one very fine exception—*The Nutty Professor*. This funny and really well-made take off on Dr. Jekyll and Mr. Hyde proves that Lewis has (had?) some genuine talent (though a look at any of his other vehicles makes one wonder why there are no other signs of it). *The Nutty Professor*, by the way, would be a good source to use in a cross-media study of Robert Louis Stevenson's famous Freudian novel.

Rental from Films Inc.

THE OX-BOW INCIDENT, 90 min., black and white, 1943.

A reasonably good Hollywood version of Walter Van Tilberg Clark's powerful anti-lynching novel (though I've always preferred to teach the book). A vindictive posse rides after some alleged cattle rustlers, captures three men and hangs them, only to find out later that the men were innocent. The movie suffers from the limitations of being filmed in a studio, particularly in light of the naturalistic descriptions in Clark's prose.

Rental from Films Inc.

THE PHANTOM OF THE PARADISE, 98 min., color, 1974.

A fast, funny version of *The Phantom of the Opera*, with elements of *Frankenstein* and *A Portrait of Dorian Gray* thrown in. Young, talented filmmaker Brian De Palma has set his horror spoof in a futuristic setting of a rock n' roll palace, and its phantom is an obscure composer who has been cheated of fame by a vicious record entrepreneur. The film has a few kinky moments and some semi-explicit sex (though it has a PG rating), but might work well with senior high students.

Rental from Films Inc.

POPI, 113 min., color, 1969.

A warm, human comedy, starring Alan Arkin as a Puerto Rican widower struggling to raise two young sons in the New York ghetto of Spanish Harlem. The film has a satirical edge as Arkin tries to have his sons pass themselves off as Cuban refugees in order to get special government benefits. Naturally, the scheme backfires, but it casts some stinging barbs at American values in the process. The film was later adapted into a TV situation comedy series.

Rental from Universal 16.

PSYCHO, 108 min., black and white, 1960.

Alfred Hitchcock's masterpiece of horror is not for the squeamish, though over the years with repeated viewings we've all come to notice the deft and subtle humor embodied in this gory

Films Inc.

Ride the High Country

film. Particularly recommended for film aesthetics and film history courses, *Psycho* is a textbook of techniques.

Rental from Universal 16.

RIDE THE HIGH COUNTRY, 94 min., color, 1962.

Director Sam Peckinpah's *Ride the High Country* poetically portrays the decline of the mythological, heroic lawman of the Old West. It stars Joel McCrea and Randolph Scott as two aging ex-marshalls sent on a mission to guard a mine payroll in the late 1890s. Their cherished free society frontier (which permeates the legend of the Old West) disappears before the two old men as they prepare for one last heroic stand. This film can be the basis for an entire English or social studies unit on American mythology. It is a gentle, highly moral movie.

Rental from Films Inc.

ROOTS, seven episodes, 90-120 minutes each, color, 1977.

This epic mini-series of Alex Haley's family geneology from Africa through emancipation made television history.

All the episodes are available as a unit or individually, for lease or rental, from Films Inc.

SAYONARA, 147 min., color, 1957.

This is an excellent film to use in a world cultures context since it beautifully documents the impact of American culture of post-World War II on Japan and vice versa. Based on a novel by James Michener, *Sayonara* depicts the love between an American Air Force officer and a Japanese actress, and the United States' military policy that forbade interracial marriage. The excellent cast features Marlon Brando as the officer.

Rental from Twyman Films.

THE SCALPHUNTERS, 102 min., color, 1968.

A very funny and exciting satirical western about a frontiersman and the runaway slave he "inherits" from the Indians. The film has a very contemporary point of view, since the slave is an academic genius who pragmatically shifts his allegiances as part of his art of survival. Extremely well acted by Burt Lancaster as the frontiersman, Ossie Davis as the slave, and Telly Sevalas as a comic villain.

Rental from United Artists 16.

THE SET UP, 72 min., black and white, 1949.

A minor classic, directed by Robert Wise, about an hour or so in the life of an aging boxer (Robert Ryan) who awaits the brutal consequences from the crime syndicate for whom he has refused to throw a fight. This film, like *High Noon*, is an example of cinematic approximation of "real time."

Rental from Films Inc., or the Museum of Modern Art.

SINGIN' IN THE RAIN, 103 min., color, 1951.

This is generally regarded as one of the finest of all Hollywood musicals, and it is also a hilarious spoof of the movie industry in the days of the early talkies. This would be a great source in a movie history course, both as a depiction of the end of silent films, and as a superb refinement of the musical genre. Directed by Gene Kelly (who also starred) and Stanley Donen.

Rental from Films Inc.

SKATERDATER, 20 min., color, 1966.

An Oscar-winning short about a group of pre-teen boys who ride around on skateboards. One of them falls in love with a pretty ten-year-old girl and must decide whether to skate with the crowd or roll off in his own direction. The film is beautifully done, without dialogue, and with a nice upbeat musical score orchestrating the youngsters' actions. Particularly recommended for upper elementary and middle school use.

Purchase or rental from Pyramid Films.

SLEEPER, 92 min., color, 1973.

I have never been a die-hard Woody Allen buff, but this science fiction spoof, which he directed and co-wrote, is a lot of fun. Although some of the gags will date quickly because of the early 70s references, the film might work well in units in both science fiction and humor.

Rental from United Artists 16.

SOME LIKE IT HOT, 120 min., black and white, 1959.

My favorite screen comedy, directed by the great Billy Wilder. The plot about two musicians who disguise themselves as women and join an all-girl orchestra to hide from a mob is violent, but very funny. Jack Lemmon, Tony Curtis, Marilyn Monroe, and especially Joe E. Brown as a tipsy old playboy are all at their comic best. The film was later adapted as a Broadway musical called *Sugar*, which was a resounding flop.

Rental from United Artists 16.

THE SORROW AND THE PITY, 244 min., black and white, 1972.

One of the finest documentary films ever made and a landmark in movie history. Marcel Ophul's four-hour-plus film about France during the Nazi occupation and Vichy regime is a brilliant combination of rare film clips and on-screen interviews and is a superb source for teachers of 20th-century history. The length of the film should not be a problem for teachers, since it actually works better when screened in sections over a period of several days.

Rental from Cinema V.

THE SOUTHERNER, 95 min., black and white, 1944.

A rarely shown, American-made film by the French director Jean Renoir. During World War II Renoir came to America and made a handful of films in Hollywood, which unfortunately were badly cut by the studios he worked for. *The Southerner* was the only American film he made that wasn't compromised by the industry. It is a realistic, somber portrait of a group of southern sharecroppers struggling for survival. William Faulkner allegedly worked on the script. This film would work very well in a unit including *The Grapes of Wrath* and James Agee's *Let Us Now Praise Famous Men* (Houghton Mifflin, 1941).

Rental from Ivy Films.

SPLENDOR IN THE GRASS, 127 min., color, 1962.

William Inge's Oscar-winning original screenplay about frustrated young lovers in the mid-America of the late 1920s has always been a favorite of adolescent audiences. There seems to be something resonant to kids about the emotions of the young couple in the film (Natalie Wood and Warren Beatty), and many teachers show the film regularly because it has that appeal. It is a particularly good stimulus for student creative writing. Complete screenplay available in Scholastic's "Literature of the Screen" series in the *Men and Women* volume.

Rental from Twyman Films or Swank Films.

THE STORY OF G.I. JOE, 100 min., black and white, 1945.

One of the finest films of the World War II era, *G.I. Joe* is based on the European correspondences of reporter Ernie Pyle and depicts the combat experiences of an army company from 1942 until 1945. Unlike many of the propagandistic movies of the period, this film is very realistic and reflects the growing disillusionment of Americans toward war by 1945 (symbolized in one scene depicting a soldier actually being carried away in a state of shock due to battle fatigue). A fine historical source.

Rental from Budget Films.

THE SUNDOWNERS, 133 min., color, 1960.

A good cinematic portrait of modern pioneer life in Australia. The plot involves the nomadic existence of a family of sheepherders on Australia's frontier, and individualistic struggles against the traditional civilization. Starring Robert Mitchum, Deborah Kerr, and Peter Ustinov.

Rental from Twyman Films or Swank Films.

SULLIVAN'S TRAVELS, 91 min., black and white, 1942.

Screen satire at its best from Preston Sturges. In 1941, despite the economic spark provided by World War II in Europe, five million people were still unemployed in the United States. The Great Depression was far from over, and *Sullivan's Travels* is an effort to portray that fact and offer a kind of solution. A movie producer named John L. Sullivan (Joel McCrea), who is known for making light comedies, decides he'll do a serious film about America's poor. When chided that he knows nothing about the subject, Sullivan sets out on a cross country odyssey to discover for himself the plight of the masses. En route he is mistakenly imprisoned in a chain gang (besides several other misadventures) and soon comes to realize that one solution to human misery is the vicarious escape provided by funny movies—the kind he has always made. The film, which has a serious side to its comedy, is a fascinating social document about America during the Depression. Highly recommended.

Rental from Universal 16 or the Museum of Modern Art.

SUNSET BOULEVARD, 110 min., black and white, 1950.

Billy Wilder's famous gothic-horror comedy about an ex-silent movie queen (Gloria Swanson), the cynical screenwriter she "keeps" as a bodyguard (William Holden), and the strange butler

Sullivan's Travels

Universal

who was once her director and husband (Erich Von Stroheim who really was a great silent film director). The film is full of inside jokes about Hollywood's past and would work very well in a film history course.

Rental from Films Inc.

TELL THEM WILLIE BOY IS HERE, 100 min., color, 1969.

A reasonably good film about the plight of the Indian, based on a true incident. In 1909 a New Mexican reservation Indian named Willie Boy (Robert Blake) killed a fellow tribesman, the father of the girl he had been denied permission to marry. Then he kidnapped the girl and ran away. Normally this would have been a minor legal matter, but the New Mexico Territory was about to be visited by President Taft, and the white citizens decided to put on a little law and order show for the President by hunting down Willie Boy. The whites become frenzied in their lust for Indian blood, and the entire incident runs amok. The film is a little too slow-moving for its own good, but it does provide a complex portrait of the incident without the usual good and bad stereotypes. Robert Redford is unusually fine as the reluctant sheriff in charge of the manhunt.

Rental from Universal 16.

THAT'S ME, 15 min., black and white, 1961.

This film originated as an improvisational theater sketch depicting a conversation between an uptight social worker (Andrew Duncan) and a Puerto Rican high school dropout (Alan Arkin). The film presents a comic confrontation of values between the two men with the social worker finally realizing that he is a walking cliche! Screenplay available in Scholastic's "Literature of the Screen" series in the *Identity* volume.

Purchase or rental from Contemporary Films-McGraw-Hill.

THE THREE FACES OF EVE, 91 min., black and white, 1957.

Here is a film that could serve as the basis for an entire unit on human psychology. Based on a true case history of a young housewife who developed three distinct personalities, this film is loaded with clinical details as it examines the causes of the woman's psychosis. Joanne Woodward won an Oscar for her portrayal of the tortured woman, and Lee J. Cobb is excellent as the psychiatrist who helps her understand the roots of her problems. This film can be extremely useful in psychology and sociology units and, since part of Eve's dilemma relates to society's rigidly defined roles for women, it would also work well in a course on women's studies.

Rental from Films Inc.

THE THREE MUSKETEERS, 95 min., color, 1974.
THE FOUR MUSKETEERS, 91 min., color, 1975.

Originally shot as a single feature film, these two episodes of the Alexander Dumas classic are delightful blends of action and slapstick humor. Directed by Richard Lester (who did those fine Beatles films in the 60s), and with an all-star cast (Michael York, Charlton Heston, Oliver Reed, Faye Dunaway, Richard Chamberlin, and Raquel Welch—for a change proving herself a fine commedienne), both films are recommended for any cross-media studies with the novel.

Rental from Films Inc.

TIME PIECE, 8 min., color, 1965.

A heavily used short film in high schools, *Time Piece* is a brilliantly edited spoof on conformity in American society. Done in syncopated animation style by Jim Henson (creator of the Muppets of Sesame Street fame), this film works very well in high school sociology courses analyzing the American value system.

Purchase or rental from Contemporary Films-McGraw-Hill.

TO BE YOUNG, GIFTED AND BLACK, 90 min., color, 1971.

Robert Nemeroff's episodic play about his late wife Lorraine Hansberry, which includes several excerpts from her works (*A Raisin in the Sun, The Sign in Sidney Brustein's Window*, and others), was videotaped for educational TV and then later converted to film. The film version is fairly stagnant to watch, but is still a moving vehicle to introduce the works of a great black American writer.

Rental from Twyman Films.

TOUCH OF EVIL, 93 min., black and white, 1958.

Orson Welles' second greatest film (after *Citizen Kane*) about a self-righteous but corrupt police chief of a sleepy town on the Mexican border and the victims he frames. This film is of particular interest to students of cinematic art for its stylistic innovations, including an incredible opening tracking shot.

Rental from Universal 16.

Universal

Touch of Evil

THE TRAIN, 113 min., black and white, 1965.

John Frankenheimer's unusual war film about a group of French underground agents who fight to rescue a trainload of art treasures stolen by the Nazis. The film makes some interesting statements about why men risk their lives and is also technically superb (there have never been train wrecks on the screen like these!). Starring Burt Lancaster, Jeanne Moreau, Michel Simon, and Paul Scofield.

Rental from United Artists 16.

TREASURE ISLAND, 88 min., color, 1950.

This is the Walt Disney, live action version of Stevenson's classic pirate tale. (There are others, but they are poor.) Robert Newton was the definitive Long John Silver (he even repeated the role in a couple of spin-offs), and the script is very close to the text of the novel. Particularly recommended for students in grades four to six, for whom there aren't many good feature films.

Rental from Films Inc.

THE TREASURE OF SIERRA MADRE, 125 min., black and white, 1948.

A legendary American film by John Huston about a trio of American prospectors in Mexico in the 1920s. It is both an adventure story and a statement on human greed. Starring Humphrey Bogart, Walter Huston, and Tim Holt. Based on the little-read but equally fine novel by B. Traven.

Rental from United Artists 16.

TWO FOR THE ROAD, 111 min., color, 1967.

I always had excellent luck with my students with this intelligent, sophisticated comedy about a modern marriage. The lives of a married couple are presented at a series of stages in their relationship, each portrayed from the point of view of a different motor trip through France. The film is also distinguished for its unique editing style. Starring Audrey Hepburn and Albert Finney.

Rental from Films Inc.

THE UNCLE SMILEY SERIES (Ecology for Children) seven color films, about 15 min., each, 1973-74.

A series of films for younger children (grades K-4) which use slapstick humor to teach about respect for the natural environment. Uncle Smiley is a lovable fat man who demonstrates several ecological dos and do nots. These films are very well made.

Purchase or rental from Learning Corporation of America.

WALKABOUT, 100 min., color, 1971.

Rapidly becoming a classroom staple, this beautifully photographed film is a particularly good source for values education units. A father goes berserk and abandons his teen-age daughter and nine-year-old son in the midst of the Australian outback (desert) before committing suicide. The children wander aimlessly in the wilderness, until an aborigine teen-ager teachers them to survive and guides them back to civilization (symbolized by a modern highway). The film ends tragically with the girl's rejection of the aborigine's friendship and his suicide. Teachers should be warned that there are very quick shots of frontal nudity that might cause some controversy.

Rental from Films Inc.

WALTER KERR ON THEATER, 27 min., color, 1970.

An excellent, made-for-the-classroom film featuring the *New York Times'* theater critic, Walter Kerr, as on-screen narrator,

Walkabout

describing the nature of modern stagecraft. The film also includes some exciting scenes from such plays as *The Importance of Being Ernest, Prometheus Bound,* and *No Place to Be Somebody.*

Purchase or rental from Learning Corporation of America.

THE WHITE DAWN, 91 min., color, 1974.

A strange and not totally successful film about the culture shock of three American whalers shipwrecked among a tribe of Arctic Eskimos. The Americans abuse the hospitality of their hosts, particularly the honored custom of wife-sharing and are ultimately punished for their crimes. This film would be good companion for *The Savage Innocents* (see page 134), despite certain stylistic ambiguities. *The White Dawn* suffered in its initial release from an R rating, though I understand that the questionable nude scene responsible for this has been cut.

Rental from Films Inc.

THE WILD CHILD, 90 min., black and white, 1970. (In French; English subtitles.)

Francois Truffaut's brilliant nonfiction film about a young nineteenth-century doctor's (portrayed by Truffaut) attempts to civilize a "wolf child." A very moving account of the actual experiments of M. Jean Itard, in many ways reminiscent of *The Miracle Worker*.

Rental from United Artists 16.

WIND, 7 min., color, 1973.

A lovely animated film about a little boy's walk through a wind-blown countryside. The wind blows, and the trees and clouds take special shapes in the child's imagination. This film would be an excellent device to get young children (K-3) to talk about their own imaginations, and it could motivate a lot of free form creative artwork.

Purchase or rental from Learning Corporation of America.

WITNESS FOR THE PROSECUTION, 114 min., black and white, 1957.

My favorite courtroom drama and a prototype of that genre. From a play by Agatha Christie, but with a few new twists of its own provided by writer-director Billy Wilder. Charles Laughton excels as the wily old defense attorney and Marlene Dietrich as the star witness.

Rental from United Artists 16.

THE WRONG MAN, 105 min., black and white, 1957.

A very low key film from Alfred Hitchcock, based on a true incident. A night club musician (Henry Fonda) is accused by eye witnesses of committing a murder. He is tried and convicted, although it is ultimately proven that the real murderer was a man with a striking resemblance to him. In the meantime his wife has a mental breakdown, and his whole way of life is shattered. A thoughtful and frightening film with great classroom potential.

Rental from Warner Brothers Film Gallery.

Selected
Bibliography

There are currently a large number of mass market film and media books available in hardcover and paperback. The great problem with too many of these, however, is their incredible low quality. I'm not sure of all the reasons, but writing style, scholarship, and even accuracy of editing generally seem at their lowest ebb in film books. They tend to take an idol worshipping, noncritical approach to their material, which, of course, appeals to film buffs but is not reliable for serious film students. Throughout the pages of this volume I have cited a number of printed works which are relevant to the content of specific chapters. Beyond those titles, there are not very many that I could add to create a resource booklist for teachers of film-oriented curriculum. Hence, what I am presenting here is a brief, highly selective bibliography of works I have found to be of some value in my own teaching.

Books for Teachers

Amelio, Ralph. *Film in the Classroom*. Dayton, Ohio: Pflaum Publishing, 1971.
Amelio is a good film scholar who addresses his classroom advice to teachers of film art and film history.

Although I don't share his approach, I find him an excellent reference source.

Kuhns, William. *Themes: Short Films for Discussion.* Dayton, Ohio: Pflaum Publishing, 1968.

A useful, loose-leaf arrangement of brief guides to popularly used shorts.

Maynard, Richard. *The Celluloid Curriculum.* Rochelle Park, N.J.: Hayden Book Co., 1971.

My own product of the 60s. (I hereby take back the statement that the film *IF* "is truly a film for today's youth." It died in my classes after I wrote that.) I'm told teachers still find the book useful.

Schillaci, Anthony, and Culkin, John, eds. *Films Deliver.* New York: Citation Press, 1970.

A fine anthology of some of the best teaching of film during the 60s.

Books for Students (texts in film and media study)

Coping with the Mass Media, Evanston, Ill.: McDougal-Littell, Inc., 1972, 1976.

Literature of the Screen: Four Thematic Volumes of Screenplays. New York: Scholastic, 1974.

IDENTITY contains: *That's Me, Loneliness of the Long-Distance Runner, Cool Hand Luke,* and *Up the Down Staircase;* POWER contains: *Mr. Smith Goes to Washington, A Face in the Crowd,* and *The Candidate;* MEN AND WOMEN contains *Splendor in the Grass, The Family Way* and *Nothing But a Man;* VALUES IN CONFLICT contains: *High Noon, The Hustler,* and *The Savage Innocents.*

Mass Communications Arts, 2 vols. New York: Scholastic, 1975.

Morrow, James, and Murray, Suid. *Filmmaking Illustrated: The Comic Filmbook.* Rochelle Park, N.J.: Hayden Book Co., 1972.

Filmmaking—Film Technique Books

Gessner, Robert. *The Moving Image: A Guide to Cinematic Literacy.* New York: E.P. Dutton, 1968.
  Still the best book of its kind.

Smallman, Kirk. *Creative Film-making.* New York: Bantam Books, 1969.

Stephenson, Ralph, and Debrix, Jean R. *The Cinema as Art.* Baltimore: Penguin Books, 1965.

Collected Criticism and Film History

Agee, James. *Agee on Film,* vol. I. New York: Grosset and Dunlap, 1969.
  Excellent, literate reviews of films of the 1940s.

Bogle, Donald. *Coons, Mammies, Mulattos, etc.: The Images of Blacks in the Movies.* New York: Bantam Books, 1973.

Haskell, Molly. *From Reverence to Rape: The Image of Women in Films.* New York: Bantam Books, 1974.

Jacobs, Lewis, ed. *The Emergence of Film Art.* New York: Lion Press, 1970.
  The best of the film history anthologies.

Kael, Paulene. *I Lost It at the Movies* (1965); *Kiss Kiss Bang Bang* (1968); *Going Steady* (1970); *Deeper Into Movies* (1973); *The Citizen Kane Book* (1973); all published by Little, Brown and Co.
  The best of the contemporary film critics and the only one consistently worth reading.

Rotha, Paul. *The Documentary Film,* 3rd ed. New York: Hastings House, 1964.

Warshow, Robert. *Immediate Experience: Movies, Comics, Theater, and Other Aspects of Popular Culture.* New York: Atheneum, 1970.
  A collection of literate essays by a late noted social critic.

Film
Distributors
Directory

Whenever possible, try to plan an entire semester's or year's schedule of films by early September. I realize the difficulty caused by unannounced schedule changes throughout the school year, but careful advanced planning means that you will probably get your first choice of films. Distributors do not have large numbers of prints of each of their films. Often by late fall popular titles such as *Cool Hand Luke, On the Waterfront, Citizen Kane,* and the like are booked up for the entire year. Most distributors will reserve a print by phone (some even let you call collect or have a toll-free number), if you follow up with a confirming letter. All distributors will furnish free descriptive catalogs of their titles upon written request.

Benchmark Films, 145 Scarborough Rd., Briarcliff Manor, N.Y. 10510. Tel: (914) 762-3838

BFA Educational Media, 2211 Michigan Ave., Santa Monica, Calif. 90404.

Budget Films, 4590 Santa Monica Blvd., Los Angeles, Calif. 90029. Tel: (213) 660-0187

Carousel Films (prints for sale only), 1501 Broadway, Suite 1503, New York, N.Y. 10036. Tel: (212) 279-6734

Charlou Films, Inc., 165 West 46th St., New York, N.Y. 10036. Tel: (212) 247-3337

Churchill Films, 662 North Roberston Blvd., Los Angeles, Calif. 90069. Tel: (213) 657-5110

Cinema V, 595 Madison Ave., New York, N.Y. 10022. Tel: (212) 421-5555

CLIO Awards (Television Commercials), 30 East 60th St., New York, N.Y. 10022. Tel: (212) 593-1900

Columbia Cinematheque, 711 Fifth Ave., New York, N.Y. 10022. Tel: (212) 751-7529

Contemporary Films-McGraw-Hill, 1221 Ave of the Americas, New York, N.Y. 10020. Tel: (212) 997-1221

Films Incorporated, Central office: 1114 Wilmette Ave., Wilmette, Ill. 60091. Tel: (312) 256-4730

Film Makers Cooperative, 175 Lexington Ave., New York, N.Y. 10016. Tel: (212) 889-3820

Grove Press Films/Cinema 16, 80 University Place, New York, N.Y. 10016. Tel: (212) 889-3820

Hurlock Cine World Film Library, 13 Arcadia Rd., Old Greenwich, Conn. 06870. Tel: (203) 637-4319

Indiana University Audio Visual Center, Bloomington, Ind. 47405. Tel: (812) 332-0211

Images, Inc., 2 Purdy Ave., Rye, N.Y. 10508. Tel: (914) 967-1102

International Film Bureau. 332 South Michigan Ave., Chicago, Illinois 60604. Tel: (312) 427-4545

International Film Foundation. 475 Fifth Ave., New York, N.Y. 10017. Tel: (212) 685-4998

Ivy Films. 165 West 46th St., New York, N.Y. 10036. Tel: (212) 765-3940

Janus Films, 745 Fifth Ave., New York, N.Y. 10022. Tel: (212) 753-7100

Learning Corporation of America. 1350 Ave. of the Americas, New York, N.Y. 10019. Tel: (212) 397-9352

Macmillan Audio Brandon Films. Main Office: 34 MacQuesten Parkway, So., Mt. Vernon, N.Y. 10550. Tel: (914) 664-5051

McGraw-Hill Films. 1221 Ave. of the Americas, New York, N.Y. 10020.

Museum of Modern Art Film Library. 11 West 53rd St., New York, N.Y. 10019. Tel: (212) 245-8900.

National Film Board of Canada (Films for sale only) 1251 Ave. of the Americas, New York, N.Y. 10020. Tel: (212) 586-2400.

New Line Cinema. 121 University Place, New York, N.Y. 10003. Tel: (212) 674-7460

New Yorker Films, 43 West 61st St., New York, N.Y. 10023. Tel: (212) 247-6110

Perspective Films, 369 West Erie St., Chicago, Ill. 60610

Phoenix Films. 470 Park Ave., So., New York, N.Y. 10016. Tel: (212) 684-5910

Pyramid Films. P.O. Box 1048, Santa Monica, Calif. 90406. Tel: (213) 395-5200

RBC Films. 933 La Brea Ave., Los Angeles, Calif. 90038. Tel: (213) 874-5050

Swank Motion Pictures. 201 South Jefferson Ave., St. Louis, Mo. 63103. Tel: (314) 531-3100

Time-Life Films, Time & Life Building, New York, N.Y. 10020. Tel: (212) 556-4020

Twyman Films. 329 Salem Ave., Dayton, Ohio 45401. Tel: (513) 222-4014

United Artists 16. 729 Seventh Ave., New York, N.Y. 10019. Tel: (212) 575-3000

Universal 16. 445 Park Ave., New York, N.Y. 10022. Tel: (212) 759-7500

Warner Brothers Film Gallery. 4000 Warner Blvd. Burbank, Calif. 91503. Tel: (213) 843-6000

Xerox Films, High Ridge Park, Stamford, Conn. 06904

Zipporah Films, 54 Lewis Wharf, Boston, Mass. 02110. Tel: (617) 742-6680

Film Title Index